Who's Driving Your Bus?

ISBN 10: 0-9711623-0-1
ISBN 13: 978-0-9711623-0-3
Library of Congress Control Number: 20001119768

Published by Sapphire Publishing
Santa Maria, CA 93544
805-478-0933
www.sapphire-publishing.com
Printed by Lightning Source, Inc., La Vergne, TN 37086

Sapphire Publishing

Dedicated To
My Clients and Readers
who allowed me into
their world.

TABLE OF CONTENTS

ACKNOWLEDGEMENTS

My heart-felt thanks go out to my beloved family of friends who have believed and encouraged my pursuit of this project. It was a blessing to have their personal and professional support in my efforts to make this book a reality to help millions. My appreciation goes out to my editor, Rita Karnopp, who helped bring alive each character through her editing style, humor and wit. And to Pashur House, for his ability to create and capture the distinct personalities of each character through his artwork.

Book Reviews

My sincere gratitude goes out to the following individuals who took time from their personal and professional lives to review my book. I appreciate each and every one of their comments regarding the content of my book. My congratulations go out to each of them in their individual efforts to continue making a difference in people's lives. Thank you for making a difference in mine.

"Cheryl's book offers valuable insights on human behavior. I recommend her book to all parents who seek a closer relationship with their children." — Annabelle Tacogue, Wife and Mother

"As a grandmother of two I've found *Who's Driving Your Bus?* to be an awakening! I only wish this book had been around to help me be a better parent." — Helen DeVoss, Grandmother

"In this age of victimization, it's refreshing to be reminded that our behavior has consequences. And that the behavior we use is the behavior we choose. I'll be recommending Cheryl's book to many of my clients." —James D. Baxendale, Ph.D., Psychologist, Certified Trauma Specialist

"This is an excellent approach to a difficult subject—our inner lives." — Betsy Rushworth, Ph.D., Clinical Psychologist

"As a school counselor, this book will be an incredible tool in counseling children how to respond appropriately to their peers. It'll help parents understand how to effectively use and improve their parenting skills. Cheryl addresses every day problems while using humorous drawings and clear explanations. Bravo!" — Mary Moore, NBCC, LPC, School Psychologist

"A wonderful, insightful, and understandable owner's manual suitable for any human being." —Robert Page, ED. D., LPC, Certified Criminal Specialist

"Anyone who is trying to gain control in their life ought to read this book." — Jerry Oliver, Ph.D., Clinical Psychologist

"Cheryl has successfully helped many of my patients make monumental transformations. I'm excited that she can now share her wealth of knowledge to a much larger audience." —Timothy J. Kosmatka, MD

"Take control of your destiny. *Who's Driving Your Bus?* is a fun read with real life analogies...everyone can identify with it." —Mary Fay, M.Ed., LCPC, Chief, Probation & Parole

INTRODUCTION

Ego Bit: *People will change when you change how you think or feel about them.*

What is an Ego Bit?

An Ego Bit is a short blurb, sometimes thoughts, on how to take control of your life to make positive changes. I hope you find individual meaning in each of them.

What did I learn from my clients?

As a Licensed Professional Counselor in private practice, I see hundreds of clients who are looking for help in many different aspects of their life. I developed a simple and practical approach by piecing together what I learned from graduate school with information shared by my clients. A typical session would start with a simple diagram to help explain my approach to therapy (See diagram 7-1). As each session progressed, my clients began to discover profound things about themselves.

In turn, I began to recognize similar patterns of questions and comments.

Why do I allow people to take advantage of me?

Why do I act like a rebellious kid around my partner?

Why am I so impatient with my children?

I feel like I have to dominate business meetings when others don't like my ideas.

I hate it when I have a temper tantrum. I'm an Adult.

I can't believe I say so many hurtful and negative things to people. I just feel awful.

I use to love to have fun; now I feel too old.

1

"She's not the fun-loving woman I married three years ago." "And he's not the kind and considerate man who asked me to marry him either." Therapist: "So who are you?"

It became clear to me they were looking for specific answers to the following questions: Why do I behave in this manner? Why do I feel this rush of emotions or say what I don't mean? My clients felt as if they had very little control over their behavior.

So who was controlling their behavior? I came to the conclusion it was five distinct characters: the Nurturing Parent, the Critical Parent, the Adult, the Responsible Child and the Rebel Child.

Each character has recognizable behaviors, thoughts, and feelings that develop from each client's environment. Consequently, these distinct characters fight for individual attention through the process I'll call internal conflict. Internal conflict occurs when, simultaneously, more than one character wants to be seen, heard, and his or her feelings validated. It's this internal conflict between characters that causes you to procrastinate or feel overwhelmed. Nonetheless, each character's unique characteristics are extremely important. You need them to help cope with different situations in every day life.

Purpose of this book

The purpose of this book is to share my knowledge that has helped thousands of people. I'll help you become an expert on you, so you can resolve your own problems. This entails teaching you how to maintain emotional balance between these five characters, so you're in control of your life. In order for you to do this, you must follow three simple steps:

Step 1: Recognize each of the five character's distinct qualities. In chapters one through five I'll introduce each character in a short story format. Chapter six I'll devote to helping you recognize descriptions of each of the character's behaviors, feelings, attitudes, beliefs, and thoughts.

Step 2: Regulate or manage your five characters to maintain emotional balance. In chapter seven, I'll explain five basic tools to help regulate each of your five distinct characters to maintain emotional balance. I'll use simple diagrams, tools, and techniques to teach self-control.

Step 3: Replace the character for the one who can achieve positive results. In chapter eight, I'll explain when and how to switch from one character to another using real life scenarios.

Throughout my book, I'll integrate humorous illustrations to help you follow the story line and different scenarios. I'm sure you'll get a chuckle or two from these delightful characters. I'll use the word "character" when I'm referring individually to the Nurturing Parent, the Critical Parent, the Adult, the Responsible Child, or the Rebel Child. And, I'll use the word "self" when I'm referring to all five characters collectively.

Who's driving your bus?

I came up with this title for my book because this is the exact question I ask my clients in therapy session. I draw a bus on my whiteboard with five stick figures (representing each of the five characters) standing next to the bus. I explain each character's personality in detail. Then, I explain to my client, "The *bus* represents *you*. The driver you choose to sit in the driver's seat will be the one who will deal with your problems. So, select the best character."

The reason I take this approach is because it gives my client a visual of himself or herself. Plus, I'm teaching them that they are ultimately responsible for the choices they make in life. I further explain, "Life's circumstances at work, home, school, or play remain outside of the bus (you). In other words, blaming others, such as your boss for work problems, your partner for relationship problems, children for family problems, or parents for personal problems, essentially makes you a *passenger* in someone else's bus."

I conclude by stating, "The only person you can control is you." I ask the client to select the best character to sit in the driver's seat depending on the outcome they want to achieve. This exercise empowers the client putting him or her in control of their *bus*.

Who is this book for?

This book is for Adults and teens from any culture and life style. I recommend an adult explain the basic concept to school-age children using the whiteboard exercise I mentioned previously in this chapter. For professionals who help or work with people on a daily basis, this book will give you a different perspective on how to use what you currently know. It's my intention to leave no one out when I say, "Who's Driving Your Bus? is for you."

Over 1.5 million people worldwide have already benefited from the basic content of this book in daily email tips on positive living, parenting, relationships, teen, and work-related problems. This includes the hundreds of clients in my private practice and readers of W. O . E ., Women Of Excellence magazine.

Is this book for me?

Do you want more effective parenting techniques?

Are you solving everyone's problems, but can't resolve your own?

Do you want better communication skills at home or work?

Are you torn between wanting to hang out at the beach or play golf instead of work?

Do you get upset or too emotional when your feelings get hurt?

If you answered "Yes" to any one of these questions, then this book is for you. Keep in mind that you're not alone. Everyone has experienced these behaviors, thoughts, and feelings at one time or another. If you follow the three steps, Recognize, Regulate, and Replace, you'll have a clearer picture of who you are, how to resolve your own problems, and how to maintain emotional balance between characters. To sum it up, this book will teach you how to get into the driver's seat of your own bus—so you can take control of your life. Let's get started!

– CHAPTER I –

THE NURTURING PARENT

Ego Bit: *You get better results with honey than vinegar.*

When you were born, God gave you your own bright, shining bus. The bus represents you as you journey through life. Each window represents openings for opportunities in which people or situations enter in and out of your life. The emergency exit (sliding door) represents an emotional, physical or mental escape known as meditations. Meditation means to engage in contemplation or reflection of personal thoughts thus detaching you from the world. There will be times you'll need to use this exit to nourish and replenish your soul's positive energy. Daily stressors in work, parenting, and relationships literally drain you of this energy. It's important to take time for you, so the time you spend with loved ones is positive.

As an infant you had no choice but to be the passenger of a parent's bus. For the purpose of this book, the word "parent" will be used synonymously to represent anyone who was responsible for your well being, even if it was only for a few minutes. They could have been your biological parents, siblings or relatives. They could also be people outside of your home such as teachers, day care providers, health care providers, and counselors.

Being in the care of these individuals taught you how to drive your own bus (control your self) through life. You learned to drive your bus by simply watching how your parents (controlled themselves) drove theirs. They taught you how to drive safely and defensively. How to obey the rules of society and remain alert to what may be around the corner. After all, a parent's job is to prepare you for all those crazy drivers on the road. They did their best to teach you how to drive your own bus by allowing you to be a passenger in their bus.

The Nurturing Parent drives his or her bus with pride and loving care. Each morning they give their bus the best oil (beverages) and fuel (food) that they can afford. They take time to wash (bath), polish (dress) and give their bus (themselves) a hug. Even when they feel they're on their last wheel (frustrated) or they're running out of fuel (exhausted), these parents are empathic, compassionate, patient, and good listeners. They're always willing to lend a helping hand to another driver on the road of life.

"Grandpa, daddy said you're the best pancake flipper in the neighborhood . "

As a passenger, in a Nurturing Parent's bus, you reaped the benefits of learning from the treatment you received. You were treated exactly as they treated their bus (themselves), which was with love and pride. They never cut anyone off (ignore or brush someone off). They would allow other drivers to squeeze in and out of traffic (putting needs of others first) kindly waving them in. They avoided potholes and bumps (negative or dangerous conditions) on the road of life by choosing serene, beautiful, and scenic roads (circumstances which yield positive rewards).

These Nurturing Parents reminded you daily how much they unconditionally loved and appreciated you for making their lives fulfilling and enjoyable. As a young child you witnessed this unconditional love by several of your Nurturing Parents. This is how you developed your nurturing ability. You knew someday, when you were old enough to have passengers in your bus, you'd treat them the same way.

CHAPTER II

THE CRITICAL PARENT

Ego Bit: *There is a fine line between criticisms and teachings; one is the truth of how you see things and the other is simply the truth.*

As a child in chapter one, you were the passenger in many different parental buses as they drove you around in life. They might have been your biological or foster parents, siblings or relatives. They might have been people outside of your home, such as teachers, day or health care providers, and counselors. Consequently, you were subjected to their personal and private problems and how they coped with them. The fact you were the passenger in their bus was beyond your control. So, you might have tried to escape emotionally or physically when things got uncomfortable. Some of you who tried relentlessly to escape were yanked back into your seat, or made to sit on his or her lap.

"It wasn't me. I stopped chewing on furniture
when I turned five. Rascal's not even two-years-old yet."

For the purpose of understanding the personalities of the five characters, I'll tell the story as seen through the eyes of a young child, Johnny. Let's begin our story about Johnny and his mother.

Our story begins with Johnny who will soon turn four-years-old. For the purpose of explaining each character in detail, Johnny is highly developed in his thinking though he's having some delay in toilet training. Pay close attention to your feelings and try to remember if a similar situation has ever happened to you.

Johnny struggled to stay in a good dream as he fought against something that had a vice grip on his shoulder. "What?" he mumbled.

"Get up! Now! I want you to dress and be downstairs in fifteen minutes."

Johnny scrunched his forehead, puzzled by his mother's strange, new behavior. "Why?" Johnny sat up in bed and rubbed his eyes for a few seconds. Then, plopped backwards onto his fluffy pillow.

"Johnny, you'd better get cracking, you have ten minutes to get your behind down here," his mother threatening from the kitchen.

His mother had never been this harsh with him before. She usually saved that harsh tone for his sixteen-year-old sister. "Okay." Johnny glanced around his room and noticed his old orange T-shirt on the floor by his feet and he gracefully slipped it over his head. Then, he searched the floor with a little more effort and discovered a pair of green shorts and quickly pulled them on. As Johnny headed for the door, his gaze settled delightedly on his heavy, hiking boots. He sat on the floor and pushed his feet into each of them. Just as he struggled to get the laces just right, his mother appeared in the doorway. Happy to have dressed so quickly, he gave his mom a big smile. "When are you ever going to learn to dress yourself and tie your own shoes?"

Johnny couldn't believe his mom had ridiculed him, he thought he'd done a good job, and fast, too. He watched as his mother rustled through his chest of drawers and tossed him blue shorts and T-shirt. She gruffly pulled off the old, orange shirt and grumpily shoved his arms into the blue one. And did the same with Johnny's shorts. He remained still as she took off his favorite boots and shoved his feet into his Velcro tennis shoes instead.

"You're getting too old for this nonsense. Now come on, you're making me late."

"But mommy, I did it fast." He noticed she hadn't heard a word he said. She hurriedly took him by the arm and led him down the hallway. "Slow down, Ma." Johnny pleaded. As he pulled his arm free from his mother grip—Johnny flew forward rolling down the last step and on to the hardwood floor. Johnny cried, more from the shock than actually being hurt.

"Get up from there. You didn't hurt yourself. Now stop that crying. You're too old to cry over a silly fall. If you weren't so difficult this morning, we wouldn't be having these problems. Now stop acting like a baby. When are you going to grow up?"

Johnny did as his mother told him, and followed her downstairs and into the kitchen. She reached for him, and plopped him into his chair at the table. He wondered where'd his kind and loving mommy had gone and felt confused. His mom placed a drink cup soundly in front of him. Johnny noticed the cover wasn't on very good. So he tried to fix it so it wouldn't spill all over him as this would make his mother more distraught than she already was with him.

"Hurry up, drink your juice while I fix you a peanut butter and jelly sandwich for breakfast."

"Okay," he said, as he reached for the cup. He gripped it firmly and pressed on the cover. It popped off landing on the floor. Leaning over, Johnny peered under the table and accidentally knocked the cup over with his elbow. He quickly looked at his mom. A tear threatened to surface, but he forced it back.

"That's it, Johnny!"

He tightened his shoulders up against his neck. His mom clutched his arm and pulled him out of his chair. Johnny said nothing, as he looked down at his tennis shoes.

"You're determined to make my morning miserable, aren't you? Well, fine. You want to be careless and drop your juice on the floor, fine. You must not be hungry. You'll find out how hungry you'll get when you don't eat your breakfast."

"It fell," he explained.

"Enough! There is no talking back in this house. We don't have time for this, Johnny. We have errands to run. Stand here while I clean up this mess. Just stand right there, don't move or make a peep!"

Johnny obeyed. He stood so still his body started to shake.

"Stay right there. I'm going to look for those damned keys!"

Johnny knew something was wrong because his mom had used one of the bad words. He felt sad that he had made his mother mad at him. Waiting for his mother to return, Johnny's sixteen-year-old sister, Sarah, hurried into the kitchen.

"Hey dude. Want a sucker?" she asked.

Johnny stared at the cherry candy in her palm. He quickly glanced around to see if his mom had returned.

"What's wrong? Cat got your tongue?" she teased.

Johnny tried to smile at her, but his body seemed too stiff to move.

"It's okay. I got fussed at, too. Mom must be in a weird mood, one I haven't seen since before you were born. I hope she chills before dinner. Anyway here, put this sucker in your shirt pocket. See? It fits perfectly. By the sound of things, you're going to be hungry in no time."

Johnny glanced at the sucker and barely noticed the tip of the stick. He smiled and said, "I like cherry the best." She ruffled his hair and he liked it.

"How about when I get home from school today we watch a movie together in my room. I'll let you pick it, okay?" she asked.

He nodded as he watched Sarah grab a banana off the kitchen counter and headed out the back door. Frightened to move, Johnny waited for his mother to return.

He didn't have to wait long. She whisked him up, rushed out to the car, strapped him into his seat belt, and impatiently backed out of the garage. Just yesterday she had been so calm, warm, and patient. He watched quietly as she pressed on the horn. Startled, he flinched from the blaring noise.

"Watch where you're going! Good grief, where'd you get your license, buddy? Do you know how to use a signal light? Can't you see I have a child here?"

Adult: *"Hello 911 ... I'd like to report my Critical Parent who's on the verge of being out of control ... Yes ... I'll advice her to take three deep breaths."*

Johnny noticed that as his mom drove, she glanced several times at him in the rear view mirror.

"Johnny, you have to learn to potty train soon, because pull-ups are too expensive to be thrown down the toilet."

Johnny thought about her comment and realized he'd never seen his pull-ups thrown down the toilet. An unusual silence made him feel jittery. His mother normally sang to the music on the radio or played his favorite sing-along CD when she drove. Today the radio and CD player were off. Again, she glanced up at him in the mirror.

"As of today, no more sleeping with Mr. Bear. You're getting too old, it stinks up your bed, plus it's falling apart."

"Not Mr. Bear!!! Oh no ... my poor bear!"

Johnny couldn't believe what he just heard. How could his mommy say such hurtful words? He sat very still; scared his mother meant what she said. No Mr. Bear? Unthinkable. It was a struggle to hold back his tears.

Bump! Thump! His mother drove over a pothole in the road. Johnny bounced up against the seat belt restraint. The tightness of the restraint made him cough making it hard to breathe. Johnny felt scared so he cried out to his mother for reassurance that he wasn't hurt.

"Stop that crying! That wasn't so big of a bump that you're hurt. Stop being a cry-baby!" Mom curtly stated.

Johnny reached into his pocket and pulled out the sucker his sister had given him. He quietly removed the plastic wrap and slid the candy into his mouth. Johnny felt some comfort from it. Just yesterday his mommy had given him hugs. Today, she hadn't given him one hug yet. This Mommy was different and Johnny didn't recognize this person. He didn't want to get to know her and he certainly didn't want to be around her. Where had his nurturing parent gone? Johnny felt closed in—trapped. All he wanted to do was run away from this stranger, but he knew he couldn't. Where would he go? If he ran away, would he find a nicer person to take care of him?

When the van stopped, Johnny looked out the side window and saw they were at the grocery store. He remained silent as his mother unlatched the seat belt on his car seat. As she leaned forward and pulled him from his seat, the stick from his sucker poked his mother in the head.

"Young man? (Silence) Where did you get that sucker? I said nothing for breakfast, and I wasn't kidding."

Johnny realized she wanted to snatch his sucker away, so he grabbed it out of his mouth before she reached it. Struggling to keep it from her grasp, he soon realized his sucker didn't have a chance. Resentful, Johnny flipped it into the air to make sure his mother didn't get it.

"All right young man. I just don't need this today!"

Johnny cringed as his mother clenched him by the shoulders with both hands and lifted him to the ground. Peeking up at her he noticed his sucker had landed in her hair. It wobbled around like a gorging horn. Horrified, Johnny watched as she reached and wrapped her palm around the sticky candy.

"Johnny, I could just scream! What am I going to do with you today? I can't take any more or this."

Johnny looked around at people watching him being scolded by his mother. He wanted to hide under the van. He glanced back up at his mother and watch in amusement as she tugged and pulled on his sucker. He wondered what all those words meant. He'd never heard some of them. After several minutes, she freed it at last. Johnny glared at it all covered with black hair. His sucker was ruined. Tears mounted, he clenched his teeth to hold them back.

"I think you need a couple of swats on the behind."

"NO! NO!" Johnny pleaded.

"You're lucky all these people are watching or else I'd smack you in a heartbeat. You've been a bad boy. Now, come on. You behave in the grocery store or I'll paddle your behind in front of everyone. You hear me?" she asked, grasping him by the arm.

Johnny nodded, then struggled to pull free of her grip.

"Stop it," she ordered.

He pulled hard, determined to run away from what now appeared to be a bulging red—eyed monster. Johnny hadn't recognized this stranger and all he could think about was how to escape. He wanted to run in search of his nurturing parent whom he thought was in the grocery store. He twisted his whole body until she released her grip; this sent him to the ground.

He jumped to his feet and made a mad dash into the grocery store. Johnny ran for his life—down the potato chip aisle. He grabbed bags of chips and tossed them on the floor behind him to slow the monster up, just like he'd seen on TV Saturday morning cartoons.

"Help!" he screeched at the top of his lungs. "The monster's going to eat me!" he added, as he flung more bags of chips. He couldn't believe no one wanted to rescue him from the child-eating monster that chased him.

"Help…this she-monster ate up my mommy and I'm next!!"

As Johnny ran around the corner past the baby food aisle, his legs tired and his lungs gasped for air. Suddenly, with one swoop of the monster's hand, Johnny found himself whisked airborne into the arms of the monster. "Let me go! Let me go!" he begged.

"Hold still."

Johnny held his breath and prepared to be eaten alive. The monster pulled him tighter to its chest, and opened its mouth wide. He cried harder than he had ever cried before.

"Honey, I'm so sorry for scaring you. Let's both calm down, okay, baby?" Johnny's mother took a few deep breaths. "Its okay, mommy is fine now. See everything is going to be okay. Please stop crying, baby. Mommy is right here. Johnny, I'm not going to punish you. Please don't run from me. Are you okay? Can I have a hug?"

It seemed the bulgy red-eyed monster had suddenly disappeared. He held still, afraid if he moved the monster would come back. He struggled to understand what he'd done to make his nurturing mom go away. He didn't ever want to do that again.

"Honey, I said I was sorry. Please stop crying," Johnny's mom pleaded. (Nurturing Parent apologizing on behalf of the Critical Parent.)

Johnny felt more bewildered than ever. He resisted his mom's hugs, not sure who had spoken. After being given a Popsicle, Johnny was eventually convinced his nurturing parent had returned.

On the ride home Johnny's mother played his favorite sing-along CD. Life took on its original bright and vibrant colors once again. The scenic drive home turned out fun as usual.

"I need proof you're my mommy."

"You know I love you, don't you?"

Johnny nodded his head and exchanged a big smile with his mother, who grinned at him through the rear view mirror.

"Hey, sweetie, would you like macaroni and cheese with hot dogs for lunch?"

"Yeah!" Johnny answered fast. He sat back, and listened to his mother as she sang his favorite song, then smiled. He felt loved again.

CHAPTER III

THE ADULT

Ego Bit: *Be prepared to stand behind the behavior you choose.*

Your Adult plays a very important role in maintaining balance. It's the control center where rational, reasonable, and logical thinking takes place through the process of "self talk." Self-talk is the conversation you have mentally with your "self." It's when you talk to your "self." The job of your Adult is to guide who, when, and how to use the remaining four characters to benefit your "self." When your four characters have something to say, it's your Adult who qualifies to speak on their behalf and *drive your bus.*

Let's continue our story about Johnny and his mother. Recall in chapter two, Johnny's mother promised to prepare his favorite meal of macaroni and cheese with hotdogs. After lunch, she put him to bed, with his bear, for a two-hour nap.

Johnny awoke as his mother gently stroked his hair. He stretched and looked up at his loving mother. "We are going to my doctor's appointment, won't that be fun?"

"Yes," he answered, then climbed onto her lap.

"Can you be on your best behavior and be my big boy?"

Johnny nodded his head and nestled into his mother's arms. "I'm going to be this many," he said, as Johnny held up four fingers.

"Yes, honey, you're almost all grown up now. Let's dress you in these nice shorts and shoes, then we'll fill your backpack with all your fun stuff," she said, adjusting the laces on his new lace-up tennis shoes.

Johnny jumped off his mother's lap and reached for his backpack. He opened it and smiled when his mother handed him a box of crayons, a freshly washed Mr. Bear, and his favorite coloring book. Another grin came across his face as his mother placed him in his car seat and doubled-checked the seatbelt lock.

"I can't believe how well you ate your lunch today. My, you still must be full."

Johnny announced, "I love mac and cheese. It's the best food in the whole world." Johnny felt his mother was back to normal.

Johnny's mother stopped at a gas station to put gas in the van. As they stood in line, in the convenience store he noticed his mother as she started to talk with the man in front of them. Johnny jerked her pant leg. "Can I have a candy bar?" he quietly asked, as he attempted to get her attention away from the stranger.

"Sure sweetheart, by the way this is Mike, an old high school friend of mine. Mike, this is my son, Johnny," she introduced.

When the man extended his hand, Johnny's mom helped place his tiny hand into Mike's. Johnny gripped his hand firmly. "Hi," Johnny said, knowing that's what his dad said when he shook hands with someone.

"Oh, dear, I forgot my wallet between the seats in the van," Johnny's mother exclaimed.

"Go ahead and get it. I'll watch Johnny for you. He can keep your place in line."

Johnny wasn't so sure he wanted to stay with this old school friend of his mother, but he agreed. He was told to select a candy bar while his mother ran outside to the van to get her wallet. So he stood next to Mike and looked over the candy bars. "Yummy! Candy!" he exclaimed out loud.

Mike knelt down to Johnny's eye level.

"You sure are a tall and athletic looking fellow. I bet you play sports just like your mother, " he said. "Do you have any brothers or sisters?"

"Yes, Sarah is my big sister."

"How old is Sarah? Is she tall like you and your mom?"

"I don't know but she's really, really tall. She's taller than my mom and plays basketball every day after school. She swims like a fish too, that's what daddy says."

"Do you go to school?"

"I stay with Miss Linda sometimes. She lives next to us."

"... so you've been a football fan for almost four years huh?"

"I see. That's a nice baseball cap. You like baseball?"

"I like football, like my daddy." Johnny decided he liked Mike and appreciated being talked to like a big kid. He felt all grown up and important, just like his big sister as he answered all the adult questions.

Johnny's mother quickly returned. "Thanks, Mike, I hope he wasn't any bother. Were you a good boy?" she asked. Johnny nodded as he glanced at the candy rack.

"Okay, pick just one," she said.

Johnny smiled as he picked a bag of peanuts. He decided he'd share them with his sister when they watched their movie.

"You've got yourself one heck of an athlete… strong grip," Mike stated, turning toward Johnny. "It was nice talking with you, Sport. Good luck to you and your dad on your football team," Mike added as he headed for the door.

"Thank you," Johnny blurted back.

They arrived at the doctor's parking lot. Johnny's mother gently lifted him to the ground, and put his pack on his back. Hand-in-hand they walked into the medical building. The large waiting room seemed scary to Johnny. Johnny clung to his mother's side.

"You have a chair here, honey," she said.

He climbed into a blue chair and watched his mother walk up to a large counter top with a lady who stood behind it.

"Beth Anderson for Doctor Reed. I'm a few minutes early as usual."

"Hi, Mrs. Anderson. Doctor Reed had an emergency so he's running about thirty minutes late. If you'll have a seat, I'll call you as soon as he returns. He told me to tell you he's sorry for the inconvenience. "

"Thirty minutes!"

Johnny noticed the change in the tone of his mother's voice. Instantly he remembered the scene from the grocery store. Would his mother turn back into the bulgy red-eyed monster? What would the monster do to the lady at the desk? Where would he run if the monster came back? He watched as his mother

"…oh no… the monster… where can I hide?"

27

took a long, steady breath. "I understand these things happen...no problem, we can wait."

Wow! No monster! Johnny couldn't help be feel relieved. He beamed and felt happy that his beloved mother hadn't left him. He knew when he grew up he wanted to be just like her. He mimicked every action his mother made. He hoped to make her proud of him. When his mother picked up a magazine, he did the same. His mother flipped a few pages, so he flipped a few pages, too. His mother crossed her legs; Johnny crossed his. Johnny copied his mother's adult behavior until the doctor's nurse called "Beth Anderson" for her appointment.

"Johnny, Mommy has to see the doctor now. I want you to sit here and color. I won't be long. Okay?" she asked.

"I can sit here," Johnny responded. He wanted to sound like a big boy, even though the thought really scared him.

"If you need to blow your nose be sure to use the tissue on the coffee table," she said, pointing to the box.

"I'll remember," he said, as he watched as his mother disappeared through a large door. He looked across the room and saw other children who played quietly on the floor. He wanted to join them, then decided to stay in his chair and color, like his mother told him to do.

It wasn't very long before Johnny felt a sneeze come on. He quickly jumped off his chair, grabbed a tissue and smashed it into his nose—nothing happened. Johnny waited a few minutes for it to happen, but it seemed to have disappeared. He noticed a little girl across the room sneeze into her hand. Immediately, he ran over and offered her his tissue. "Bless you!" he said. Johnny walked back to his chair and heard an adult who commented, "What a polite young man." (Let's overlook that he offered a partially used tissue. After all he's only four.)

"Do you need to go to the bathroom, young man?" A female voice asked in a nurturing tone. Johnny looked up to find the lady from behind the counter looked down at him. "No, I already went potty at my house…and I have pull-ups, see!" He lifted his shirt so she could see the tops of his zoo animal pull-ups.

"Those are really nice. Would you like a glass of water?" she asked as she placed a cup on the counter.

"Yes, please, I'm really thirsty." Johnny reached for the small paper cup and gulped down every drop of water in it. "Thank you," he said, as he handed the empty cup back to her. He returned to his chair and continued to color.

It wasn't very long before his mother returned. "Hi, there. That's a nice job of coloring," she commented.

"Thank you," Johnny replied, happy to see her again. He watched as she picked up her magazine and placed it neatly on the table. Johnny took his magazine and placed it on top of hers. He packed his coloring book, Mr. Bear, and crayons back in his pack without being told.

"The receptionist told me you acted very grown up and you even handed a little girl a tissue. I'm so proud of you!" His mother said with pride in her voice. Johnny grinned from ear to ear. He liked feeling all grown up. It made him happy when his mother was proud of him.

CHAPTER IV

THE RESPONSIBLE CHILD

Ego Bit: *Have you hugged your inner child today?*

Your Responsible Child expresses and feels emotions. It is fun loving, and creative. Any time you get emotional about a particular situation, think about how old you feel. Sometimes your feelings trigger emotions when you were a child, teen, or young adult. Some of my clients claim to feel as young as six years old and so they behave as if they are six when expressing feelings.

Let's continue our story of Johnny and his mother at the doctor's office. Johnny learned to manage his behavior without the watchful eye of his mother. He also learned good behavior earned him praise.

"Can we come back here again, Mommy?" Johnny asked. He liked when his nurturing parent patted him on the head.

"Sure. I'm so proud of your behavior."

Johnny wanted to act like a little Adult (his Responsible Child) for the rest of the day. Excited to be home, Johnny jumped up-and-down. "Mommy, can Jackie come over and play?" he asked, as he wondered if his friend next door was home.

"Since you've been so good, yes, I think it would be nice for you to play with Jackie."

Johnny waited while his mother dialed Jackie's number, then handed him the phone. "Hi, Mrs. Parker. Can Jackie come over to play? Please?"

"Is this Johnny?" she asked.

"Oh, yes, it's me," he answered quickly. In his grown-up voice he added, "I'll share my toys with her and I'll give her a tissue if she has a runny nose." He hoped Jackie's mother would say yes.

"I suppose that would be okay. I'll walk Jackie across the street right now, so you go to the front door and let her in."

"Oh, good! I will! I mean . . . thank you." Johnny met Jackie at the door and took her to the living room to play. He dumped out the blocks so they could build a castle for the princess doll Jackie brought. They even played trucks for a while.

"You've played so well together, but now it's time for Jackie to go home," Johnny's mother explained.

Johnny reached over and gave Jackie a hug (showing his nurturing side). "Maybe you can come back and play tomorrow?" Jackie nodded and waved goodbye.

Johnny ran out to the back yard to play on his swing set. He pumped his legs hard, and kicked his feet toward the clouds. Without is playmate, he felt an onset of loneliness.

"Hey, Sweetie, I'm up here. Here I am, on your slide."

Johnny cranked his head around as far as he could to find his mother's voice. He couldn't believe his eyes. His mom sat on the top of his slide. She looked silly and too big for it. "Are you going to play with me?" he asked, not sure his mother would be his new playmate.

"Nah-nah nah-nah-nah, you can't get me," she taunted in a kid's voice.

Johnny jumped out of his swing and ran after the five-year-old mother in a thirty-five-year-old body. Johnny laughed as his mother acted just like Jackie when he chased her in the yard. Johnny screamed with excitement while he chased his mother through the water sprinklers and into the wading pool.

"Nah-nah nah-nah-nah," Johnny teased back, as he dove at his mother. They wrestled in the wet grass as they both laughed and tickled each other. "Stop or I'm going to wet my pants!" Johnny cried.

"Me, too," his mother exclaimed.

Johnny had so much fun with his mother.

– CHAPTER V –

THE REBEL CHILD

Ego Bit: *It's the manner in which you rebel, that wins respect from others.*

This chapter will introduce the Rebel Child who has a unique set of characteristics. These characteristics are essential to maintain balance of the overall child character. This character is unique in that what you think, say, or do will be completely different from another person's rebellious behavior. This is due to individual childhood experiences.

Let's continue our story as Johnny has witnessed his mother transform into a Responsible Child as she teased and tickled him in the backyard.

Johnny laughed as he chased his mother around his swing set in the back yard. He giggled when his mother dug her fingers into his waistline. "Stop," he screamed, between uncontrollable giggles.

He pushed his small fingers into this mother's waist, and she screamed, "Stop, I can't take anymore."

Johnny grabbed a handful of his mother's shirt and attempted to pull her down to the ground. He heard the material tear and quickly let it go.

"Stop it! Look what you've done to my new shirt!" his mother screamed.

Johnny froze. He stared up at his mother. Who was she? Fear that the bulgy, red-eyed monster had returned forced Johnny to take several steps back. He waited, listened, and watched.

"I'm sorry mommy," Johnny said, his voice barely above a whisper.

"You have to learn to respect other people's belongings. Haven't I tried telling you that time and time again? Do you ever listen? Damn, it's ruined, Johnny." She screamed, stomping her foot on the grass.

His mother's Rebel Child had thrown a temper tantrum right before his eyes. Where had his fun-loving playmate gone? He watched as this Rebel Child continued to yell and scream words that he was told never to use.

"I said I was sorry mommy," Johnny pleaded.

He watched in horror while the Rebel Child of his mother grabbed Mr. Bear up off the ground. Before he could blink, she ripped its little pajamas off in one tug.

"See! What do you think of that?" The Rebel Child of his mother screamed then tossed Mr. Bear to the ground.

Johnny cried as he picked up his beloved bear. The Rebel Child of his mother pushed her red face toward his. His mother's aggressive behavior made Johnny shiver.

"Now you know how it feels."

Johnny felt utterly confused and bewildered. It had been so much fun, but now he wished he'd never played with his mommy. He felt the need to hide before something worse happened.

"I won't do anything like that again," Johnny promised. Now he laid and shivered on the wet grass as he cried his tears into Mr. Bear's chest. Johnny hoped he'd get the attention of his mother's Nurturing Parent.

"Baby, please don't cry, I didn't mean to scare you. Mommy is having a very bad day. I'm angry with your Daddy and I feel so sad. I've been taking it out on you and that's not right. Honey, please forgive me." (His mother hadn't told her son that his Daddy had moved out of the house. That they had talked about divorce. That nothing would be the same again. That she had a broken heart. She wasn't about to unload on her four-year-old.)

Johnny hadn't shied away from the gentle hand that rubbed his shoulder. He lifted his face from Mr. Bear and watched tears roll down his mother's cheeks. When she extended her arms toward him, Johnny moved into her embrace.

"I'm sorry, my little man. We'll find a way to make it better, don't you worry. Mommy just needs a good cry right now."

Johnny continued to hug his mother and gently patted her on the back. "Mommy, I love you."

His mother's Responsible Child looked down at Johnny and smiled.

– CHAPTER VI –

RECOGNIZE

| Adult | Rebel Child | Nurturing Parent | Responsible Child | Critical Parent |

Ego Bit: *Self-love involves humility, openness, and forgiveness.*

Before you can recognize any of your five distinct characters you must be familiar with their individual behaviors, feelings, attitudes, beliefs, and thoughts. Behaviors a re manners in which you conduct yourself. Feelings are positive or negative emotional reactions. Attitudes are feelings or emotions toward something that is a fact. Beliefs are convictions of truth or faith. Thoughts develop from intentions, plans or ideas in your mind.

Nurturing Parent -
Now that you have an idea what behaviors, feelings, attitudes, beliefs, and thoughts are, let's do a quick exercise on getting to know your nurturing side.

Read the following:

1. List your nurturing behaviors you'd have if you agree to care for a young child or ill person.

2. List your feelings while taking care of a young child or ill person.

3. List your attitude while spending quality time with a young child or ill person.

4. List your beliefs about caring for a young child or ill person.

5. List your thoughts about people who care for children and the sick.

Write your answers in the space below.

1.

2.

3.

4.

5.

Good Job! In addition to what you wrote, here are other recognizable characteristics to be considered about your Nurturing Parent.

Behaviors are supportive, patient and kind in general. Your gestures include non-sexual touch such as hugs, pats-on-the-back, hair ruffling, high-fives, a wink, or a warm smile. You might kneel to make eye contact with children. You could nod your head to show acknowledgement when someone is speaking to you. You make every effort to listen attentively and ask pertinent questions. You ask if there's anything you can do to help, and in some cases, you might just help without asking. Your external or internal tone of voice is soft, soothing, and gentle.

Feelings relate to unconditional love and compassion. Here is a list of feeling words you can associate with your Nurturing Parent:

Active Listener	Loving	Non judgmental
Helpful	Caring	Proud
Warm	Giving	Concerned
Sympathetic	Understanding	Generous
Considerate	Teaching	Thankful
	Forgiving	

The attitude of your Nurturing Parent is compassionate, prideful, and supportive.

Beliefs about family and loved ones are in thoughts and comments using the following. When praising you can say, "Great effort!" To encourage someone a simple, "You can do it!" works quite well. Saying, "I can tell you're proud of yourself," is a good way to express pride. Offer someone hope by saying, "You'll get another opportunity." And of course, show support by offering, "I'm behind you all the way!" An expression of unconditional love sounds like this, "I love you no matter what!"

When you use your Nurturing Parent to communicate either verbally or physically to another human being, you're putting the needs of others before your own. When you conduct yourself in this manner recognize it's your Nurturing Parent who's driving your bus.

Critical Parent –

Getting to know your Critical Parent is somewhat of a humbling experience, because it requires a tough skin on your part. Don't sweat it. You're not the only person who'd rather not acknowledge their Critical Parent. Having a Critical Parent is what makes us imperfect human beings. Please take a few minutes to complete this exercise.

"The wings aren't level ... can't you see I'm too busy to help you?"

41

1. List your behaviors at work if a co-worker receives a promotion over you.

2. List your feelings about the co-worker.

3. List your attitude towards your supervisor and job.

4. List your beliefs about people who move up the corporate ladder in this manner.

5. List your thoughts about what you'll do next.

Write your answers in the space below.

1.

2.

3.

4.

5.

Congratulate yourself for your honesty and humbleness! This exercise is easier said than done. Not many people go around bragging, let alone acknowledging, how stern or critical they can be. It's easier to sweep it under the carpet and hope they never behave that way again.

Along with your descriptions, the following are other unique characteristics important in helping you recognize your Critical Parent.

Behaviors are strict, meticulous, and authoritarian. Your gestures may include finger pointing, or finger shaking, and shaking your head "No." Unknowingly, you might stand with your hands on your hips with your arms cross. You're facial expressions might be stern or you might offer an alpha-wolf stare (a stare into the eyes of the other person until they turn away). Your external or internal tone of voice will, most likely, be a notch or two above the normal tone of conversation. Be aware, this conversation will be abrupt and direct.

Feelings relate to superiority, intolerance, and perfection. Here is a list of words to associate with your Critical Parent:

Always Right	Overwhelmed	Uneasy
Overbearing	Disappointed	Preoccupied
Unforgiving	Irritated	Discouraging
Rigid	Uncompromising	Interfering
Finicky	Stressed	Tired
	Harsh-Disciplinarian	

The attitude of your Critical Parent is the feeling of superiority over others. Because of this feeling, the Critical Parent expects absolute obedience. When your Critical Parent does not receive this, they feel a loss of control. In order to gain back control, your Critical Parent will make idle threats or show conditional love.

Beliefs regarding superiority and control are in thoughts and comments using the following. When expressing impatience, "I can't take it anymore!" Example of threats would be, "Just wait until I tell your father what you did!" If you're being critical, you might say, "I expect more information in this report." It would be insensitive to say, "I don't care about why you're late." "Who cares what you have to say," would be an uncaring comment or thought. "It's my house; so I make the rules!" is an example of being dictatorial. And to set extremely harsh boundaries you might say something like, "Do as I say or else!"

In chapter two, the Critical Parent wakes Johnny in the morning in a unloving manner. The Critical Parent shames and nit-picks him as he attempts to dress, walk down the stair, and spills juice. Note: The Nurturing Parent of Johnny's sixteen-year-old sister, Sarah, consoles and empathizes with him. She gives him a sucker to eat later and invites Johnny to watch television with her after school.

Next, the Critical Parent drives impatiently to the grocery store and continues to question and threat Johnny. A struggle for control occurs when the Critical Parent and Johnny struggle for his sucker, which eventually lands in the Critical

Parent's hair. Johnny runs to escape from what appears to be a "bulging, red-eyed monster" (Critical Parent).

Johnny's mother probably didn't realize she is teaching her son Critical Parent behaviors. As do most parents, until the day comes when their child demands they, "Shut up," or slaps or kicks them.

When you use your Critical Parent to communicate, either verbally or physically, with another human you're suggesting superiority over them. When you conduct yourself in this manner, recognize it's your Critical Parent who's driving your bus.

Adult -

Adult: *"Just relax, I'm in charge of rational thinking and will take your opinions into consideration."*

You can easily recognize your Adult by paying close attention to what you consider to be your business or work self. Your business can take place either at home, in the office, or at school. Please take a few minutes to complete this exercise.

1. List your behaviors when conducting business at home, office, or school.

2. List your feelings while discussing problems with coworkers.

3. List your attitude when you're in charge of finding a solution.

4. List your beliefs about resolving problems in a rational, logical manner.

5. List your thoughts about people who remain calm during a crisis.

Write your answers in the space below.

1.

2.

3.

4.

5.

Great Job! Here are additional characteristics that will help you recognize your Adult.

Behaviors are courteous, respectful, and responsible. Your gestures comprise of hand shaking, head nodding, and eye contact. Your open body stance is confident to encourage approachability and diplomacy. Your external or internal tone of voice is calm, cool, and positive. Feelings relate to rational, logic, and confidence. Here is a list of words you can associate with your Adult:

Appreciative	Secure	Effective Listener
Reasonable	Calm	Eloquent Spokesperson
Sensible	Content	Capable
Good	Trusted	Worthy
Cheerful	Knowledgeable	Understood
Problem Solver	Comfortable	Loyal
Valuable	Competent	

The attitude of your Adult is one of being in control of ones life. There is a display of confidence and maturity.

Beliefs about control and finding "win-win" solutions are in thoughts and comments such as, "I'd like to hear how you feel about this." Evoke confidence by commenting, "I know you can handle this." "Let's see if we can work this out so we're both satisfied," is an example of mediator language. If you want to be rational, you could say, "Please explain slowly, so I can understand your side of the story." You can address being responsible with a sentence like: "I take full responsibility for what happens." And, if you wish to express obedience to yourself, then internalize your self-talk to say something like: *The traffic light is red, I'm just going to have to be late for my meeting.*

In chapter three, the Adult plays a significant role. Johnny's mother woke him from his nap in a pleasant manner. She verbally reinforces his ability to be a grown-up by telling him he is her "big boy." While standing in line to pay for gas, Johnny's mother introduces him in an Adult manner to her friend, Mike. While his mother went out to retrieve her wallet, Mike asks Johnny questions that elicit Adult responses.

While Johnny is at the doctor's office, he mimics his mother's Adult behaviors. When he hears a young girl sneeze, he offers her a tissue (oops! his tissue) and blesses her. When his mother returns, she positively reinforces him by appreciative comments for his Adult behavior. Johnny receives more positive reinforcements when his mother relays positive comments made by the nurse and bystanders.

Johnny's mother may not realize the importance of her role for teaching her son Adult behaviors. As a matter of fact, most parents teach instinctively, without giving much thought to the process. It's natural to teach offspring to fend for themselves.

How each parent chooses to teach is a matter of preference. There are several different schools of thought. Here are some examples of behaviors taught to young children with little or no effort: answering and talking on the phone, saving money, and blessing someone. We also teach behavior when we speak in full sentences, pray, and say, "excuse me," "please," and "thank you."

In addition, children are given small Adult responsibilities such as picking up their toys, feeding or dressing themselves. When they complete a grown-up task a child gets positive reinforcement by being told how grown-up they are.

Growing up, you were no different than any other child. Every child likes to hear compliments, especially about being grown-up. The more compliments (attention) you receive, the more you mimic your parent's Adult behavior.

When you use your Adult to communicate to another human being, either verbally or physically, you're showing respect. When you conduct yourself in this manner, recognize it's your Adult who's driving your bus.

Responsible Child –

"Roses are red... violets are blue... "

You'll recognize your Responsible Child by paying particular attention to your happy-go-lucky, creative, and emotional self. Your happy-go-lucky self hasn't a care in the world and enjoys doing fun creative activities such as sports, hobbies, or acting. Your emotions go from one end of the spectrum to the other. One minute you're full of excitement and the next minute you can cry yourself to sleep. The Responsible Child can be difficult to recognize. Please take a few minutes to complete the exercise.

1. List your child-like behaviors when you're playing sports or hobbies.

2. List your feelings when you're expressing yourself through creative activities such as poetry, writing music, art or acting.

3. List your attitude about people who cannot relax and have fun.

4. List your beliefs about showing and expressing emotions.

5. List your thoughts about adults or children who experience either physical, sexual, or emotional abuse.

Write your answers in the space below.

1.

2.

3.

4.

5.

Excellent! You did it! Additional characteristics to help you recognize your little Adult are as follows:

Behaviors are playful, creative, and spontaneous. Your gestures include laughing, crying, and playful teasing. You'll engage in friendly hugs or pats on the back, kisses, smiles, and innocent flirting. Your external or internal tone of voice is cute, whiney, and innocent (child like). You'll communicate in either a loud, soft, or singsong voice.

Feelings relate to joy, sadness or fear. Here is a list of words you can associate with your Responsible Child:

Affectionate	Innocent	Shy
Happy	Adorable	Insecure
Scared	Friendly	Beautiful
Indecisive	Playful	Excited
Curious	Loving	Needy
	Cute	

The attitude of your Responsible Child comes from the yearning to be have love and acceptance. Because of this, you'll try to avoid rejection at all costs.

Beliefs regarding love and acceptance are in thoughts and comments using the following expressions. Expression of fear is in the sentence, "I worry when you come home late." You can express love and security by saying, "When I'm with you, I feel safe and secure." Sadness can reflect in a comment such as, "I'm in a deep depression about moving to a new city." "I'm so grateful for having you in my life," is an expression of joy. And you can relay affection by saying, "I'm so thankful you're in my life. I love you. You're my best friend."

In chapter four, Johnny uses his little Adult to invite Sarah to play. He greets, plays fairly, and shares his toys with her. He thanks Sarah for visiting and extends a hug goodbye as Sarah goes home. As Johnny sits on his swing set, he feels feelings of loneliness. However, within moments he is feeling joy over the discovering that his mother's Responsible Child is eager to play with him.

Johnny's mother didn't realize she was role-modeling ways to tease, tickle, and splash in the wading pool. Johnny learns from his mother's Responsible Child what is acceptable child behavior.

This type of teaching is a natural, instinctive process all humans do with little or no thought. Joking and laughing is one of the best methods of teaching any adult or child.

While you are expressing emotions and behaviors in this chapter, recognize it's your Responsible Child who's driving your bus.

Rebel Child -

You can easily recognize your Rebel Child by paying attention to your aggressive and selfish behaviors (self-centeredness). This part of your child possesses both negative and positive characteristics. It's internal voice sounds like a headstrong, daring, and competitive teenager. Your Rebel Child has a passionate drive to engage in high-risk activities such as skydiving, white-water rafting, or drag racing. This would include aggressive type sports such as football, soccer, tennis, and fencing. Your Rebel Child will partake in irresponsible behavior such as drinking, smoking, or using illegal drugs. The Rebel Child will provoke violent behaviors in others.

Please take a few minutes to complete the exercise.

1. List sports and/or job that relate to activities that require high-risk or aggressive behaviors.

2. List your feelings while you engage in these high-risk or aggressive activities.

3. List your attitude while partaking in these risky or aggressive activities.

4. List your beliefs about people who take risks in life.

5. List your thoughts about people who take risks or use aggressive behavior to get what they want.

Write your answers in the space below.

1.

2.

3.

4.

5.

Bravo! Here are more characteristics to help you recognize your Rebel Child.

Behaviors can be self-centered, selfish, and unruly at times. Your gestures aim at overpowering someone in order to get what you want. You'll use negative teasing, back talk, and overtly disobey authority. You'll have paranoia, a quick-temper, and temper tantrums. You'll outwardly lie, cheat, and run away. You'll engage in hurtful gossip and may use excessive amounts of drugs and alcohol. Your external or internal tone of voice is obnoxiously rude and loud. You'll communicate by yelling and screaming to get your point across.

Feelings relate to fury, passion or intensity. Here is a list of words you can associate with your Rebel Child:

Angry	Hostile	Unappreciated
Hateful	Annoyed	Impatient
Touchy	Distrustful	Brave
Outraged	Stubborn	Difficult
Belligerent	Provoked	Resentful
	Contemptuous	

The attitude of your Rebel Child is cocky. He/she may sound like this, "Who gives a crap?" "What ever!" or "I'm out of here!"

Beliefs about aggressiveness and power are in thoughts and comments using the following expressions. "Leave me the hell alone!" is an expression of anger. If you're feeling revengeful you might say, "What comes around goes around." If you're feeling stubborn you'd most likely say, "I don't want to! I don't care what happens to me!"

Also, you can express resentment in the comment, "No one in this damn house appreciates me! I'm out of here!" If you're feeling distrustful and paranoid you might say, "I'm sure you're going to hurt me." And your self-talk might be, *"I don't care who doesn't believe in my abilities. I'm going to keep on trying!"*

In chapter five, Johnny accidentally rips his mother's blouse, and without warning she became an angry, aggressive Rebel Child. While Johnny apologizes profusely, his mother switches back to her Responsible Child, who openly expresses feelings of remorsefulness. When Johnny sees his mother's sad child, he brings out his Nurturing Parent to comfort her.

Johnny did not realize at that moment that he is now the Nurturing Parent and his mother is the Responsible Child. Though his mother probably didn't anticipate her Rebel Child showing her self, she unfortunately is the role model on how to use aggression.

Yes! This behavior will repeat itself. Each time Johnny learns a new behavior, so he'll eventually test boundaries with his sister or another person. Just as Johnny learns positive behaviors and emotions, he too will learn negative behaviors and emotions.

Don't worry. It's important to have a certain amount of rebellious personality to maintain balance. This interaction between Johnny and his mother is a natural process of teaching offspring to "toughen-up" a little. When you express emotions and behaviors in a rebellious manner, recognize it's your Rebel Child who's driving your bus.

REGULATE

Ego Bit: *Self-control begins with self-respect.*

"Today is our anniversary... so I'll need your help. Nurturing parent, I need you to listen attentively. Responsible child, I need you to be fun and show emotions. I'll make dinner reservations, buy a gift, and call a baby sitter. Rebel child and Critical Parent, I won't need your help on this play."

Now that you know how to recognize each of the five characters, this chapter will teach you how to regulate them using five basic tools. When you regulate them you're achieving emotional balance. Emotional balance occurs when none of the other characters dominate your personality with the exception of your Adult.

Diagram 7-1 represents emotional balance of an individual Note the parent and child characters are symmetrically proportionate to each other. The Adult is much larger than the rest because it serves as the command center for the "self." This command center houses all rational, logical, and intellectual thinking.

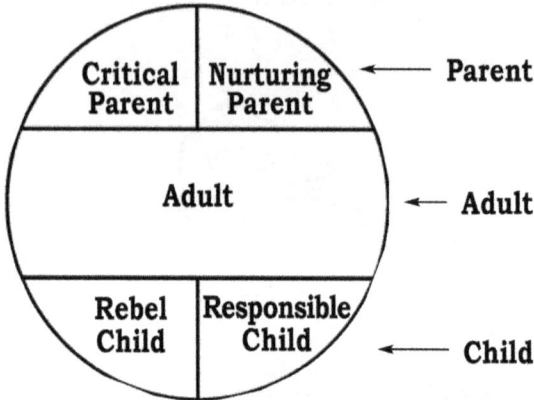

Diagram 7-1

What tools do I need?

1. Self-Reflection is taking a moment to do a self-assessment. The journey of self-discovery begins with laughing at your self. The purpose of this tool is to accept both the positive and negative aspects of who you are. Only then can you get on with the business of living a fun, exciting, and prosperous life. This requires complete honesty and a good dose of humility.

If you did not complete the exercises in chapter six, please take few minutes to do so. If you're still uncertain, ask a close friend or relative to do a personal inventory on you. Ask them to point out what your strengths and weaknesses are in relationships, at work, and at home. Ask them what your positive or negative personality traits are. Ask how you solve problems at home and at work. Ask how you discipline your children. Do not defend or rationalize their answers instead, embrace and acknowledge this truth. Take an honest, personal inventory of yourself so you'll have a clearer picture of who you truly are.

2. Adult Self-Talk is the key tool for gaining control over unnecessary behavior. *What is self-talk?* Self-talk is what you say out loud or think to your "self." It's confident, logical, and rational dialogue that guides you to do and say what is right. It speaks on behalf of your four other characters. In the following chapters, I will italicize text to represent the inner voice or self talk. Just as the picture shows at the beginning of this chapter, think of your Adult's self-talk as a coach calling plays for a football or women's soccer team. The remaining characters are the team players.

As coach, your Adult's job is to provide clear leadership. You do this by giving mental commands to bring the team players together as one. This means you must know the strengths and weaknesses of each team player. And, because each team player has their own set of experiences, it'll be up to your Adult to put in the best team player or players in the game of life. Result? You are what you say or think.

3. Emotion Regulation is expressing your feelings through gestures, tone of voice or vocabulary in a controlling manner. In other words, allowing your Adult to communicate how you feel about a problem in a calm rational manner. Result? You'll be able to express how you feel instead of acting out how your feel. You'll communicate more openly.

4. Stop Messages are internal commands meant to stop, neutralize or interrupt unnecessary inner dialogue between characters. After each stop message follow it by a positive self talk statement about the behavior you are trying to control.

For example:
- *Stop before I say something rude. I will take a moment to think before I speak.*

- *Stop nagging. I will be careful of how I remind others of things to be done.*

- *Stop. Calm down. I'm a calm and relaxed person.*

- Stop being defensive. It's not personal.

- Stop thinking of what could, would or should happen. Stay in the here and now.

- Stop. Take a moment to get in control. I can handle this problem.

- Stop. Take a deep breath. I can think this problem through in a calm manner.

- Stop imagining something is wrong. I'm confident things are fine.

- Stop. Walk away if you need to. I'm in control of what happens here.

- Stop being paranoid. I will gather the facts.

To gain control of your four other characters, it's essential to use these statements as part of your Adult self-talk. Result? You'll talk yourself into a calm, rational thinking mode.

5. Visualization means being able to see yourself in each of your five distinct characters. Picture in your mind what your Nurturing Parent, Critical Parent, Adult, Responsible Child and Rebel Child look like. Result? Pictures are worth a thousand words. Seeing yourself behaving in each character will help you regulate accordingly.

In addition, there are two important rules to help you regulate your "self." **First**, get rid of the word "should". Each time you include *should* in your vocabulary you create guilt or undue pressure. This is a word used by your Critical Parent. Make the decision to exclude this word forever; it's useless. **Second**, accept mistakes from others and yourself. Every human being makes mistakes. It's that simple. Logically thinking, no one is perfect. Store this fact in your mind and remember it.

Let's review these five basic tools to help you regulate to maintain balance.

1. Self-Reflection — to help you recognize positive and negative aspects about your self.

2. Adult Self-Talk — to help you gain control over unwanted behavior.

3. Emotion Regulation — to help you express emotions in a calm, rational manner.

4. Stop Messages — to help you neutralize inappropriate behavior.

5. Visualization — see yourself as an emotionally balanced individual.

Now that you know the five basic tools, let's discuss how to regulate each of your five distinct characters. This simply means learning how to control when and how to use your skills when you need them. I'll reintroduce each character, using the five basic tools so you have an idea of how to use each tool.

Nurturing Parent

Self-Reflection: If you did not complete the exercise in chapter six, take a few minutes to do so. This self-reflection exercise will help you develop an appreciation of what your nurturing self is really like. It's important that you're able to recognize when you're using your Nurturing Parent.

Adult Self-Talk: Beliefs on how you can express your thoughts and comments to be a nurturing person. For example, say out loud or think: I am a nurturing person. Be confident in your abilities so when the time comes to use your nurturing skills you can talk yourself into handling the circumstance.

Emotion Regulation: Knowing when to turn the nurturing person "on" or turn your nurturing person "off" is equally important. If you're overly nurturing i.e. your Nurturing Parent is always in "on", someone can easily take advantage of you. It's a good idea to practice nurturing gestures.

Prior to making contact with someone, say out loud or think about what it is you want to discuss. Here are a few nurturing self-talk examples: *Today when my daughter comes home late from school, I'm going to give her a hug, be an active listener, and ask pertinent questions as why she's late. I'll explain how it makes me feel when I don't know where she is. I'll ask her for ideas on how we can solve this problem.*

Here's another example: *This afternoon when my partner comes home late from work again, I'll greet him with tender loving kissed, kindly ask how things were at work, and listen compassionately. I'll relay my feelings without placing blame or guilt. I'll ask what I can do to help.* These statements are meant to be nurturing, but not smothering to the point of suffocating. Be careful not to baby someone constantly or you'll end up taking the mother role, and they'll assume the child role.

Practice the use of a nurturing tone of voice. Say out loud or think the following: *This evening when my daughter begins to whine about her bed time, I'll kneel down at eye level and say, "I know it's difficult to go to bed when there is so much going on. It's okay to cry and be upset. I'll help you get ready for bed." Or, I'll say, "I love you, even though I'm upset with your behavior right now."* Again, being nurturing doesn't mean you have to give in to anyone. It means you show compassion while using your Adult to maintain control over your emotions.

Stop messages: Use stop messages to help you maintain focus on being nurturing. Any distractions usually come from your Critical Parent or Rebel Child in the form of internal conflict.

What happens is that while you're concentrating on what to say to be compassionate, the voice of your Critical Parent enters to say something negative. This is meant to distract you or change your mind. For example: *I'm sorry to hear about your purse getting stolen from your car.* Enter the Critical Parent: *How many times did I tell you to lock your car? You deserve what you get.* (Use a stop message here and follow by a positive self-talk statement.) Enter the Nurturing Parent: *I'm sure your insurance covers your things. Can I do anything to help you?*

Visualization: Visualize your "self" as being kind, compassionate, and understanding. Pick a nurturing person you knew as a child as your role model, and keep that image in your mind. You'll be more apt to behave as if you were that nurturing person. (See diagram 7-2.)

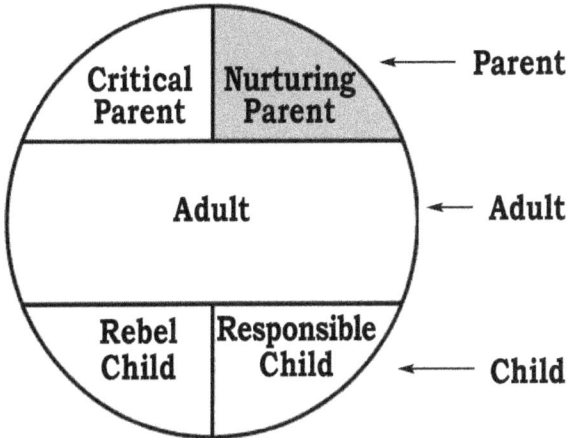

Diagram 7-2
The Nurturing Parent represents half of the total parent.

Critical Parent

Self-Reflection: Love thyself. Please take a few minutes to complete the exercise in chapter six, if you haven't already.

This self-reflection exercise does require a good dose of humbleness and self-compassion. It may be difficult to accept your critical "self" but the fact remains we ALL have these characteristics. Having a clearer picture of this side of you will help you have a better understanding of people around you.

Adult Self-Talk: Once you can accept the fact that you have a tendency to be over bearing now and then, it'll be easier to effectively use your overly assertive skills to achieve positive results. Practice saying or thinking: *In order to successfully manage my Critical Parent I'll give up power for control and delegate responsibilities to my Adult.* In other words, the less you use these critical characteristics, the more your Adult is in control. That's not to say you'll never have the need to use your Critical Parent.

Emotion Regulation: Use self-control when you feel the urge to put down or criticize someone. Allow your Adult to think through up and coming events in a rational manner. For example: *During family gatherings, I realize I tend to be bossy* (self-reflection). *If I start to lecture my little sister* (recognition), *I'll STOP immediately* (stop message). *I'll imagine I've left my Critical Parent, who sounds like my Aunt Shannon, home cleaning the garage* (visualization). *I'll speak to my sister with the respect I'd give a coworker* (Adult).

Here is another example of how to use self-talk to gain self-control. I realize I'm nagging when I constantly remind my teen-age daughter to clean up her room (self-reflection and recognition). *Today, I'll stop* (stop message). *Mentally get a grip. I'll calmly talk with her. I'll send my Critical Parent outside for a break* (visualization). *I'll ask my daughter out to lunch so we can share ideas on how she can keep her room tidy* (Adult).

Knowing what gestures you make will help you manage them to practice self-control. If you aren't aware of them, ask a close friend or relative to give you detailed examples. Ask them to mimic what your body language looks like using their hands, arms, and facial expressions. You must have tough skin, because chances are they may over-exaggerate your body language. Don't defend or make excuses, just laugh, smile, and thank them for their help.

Once you can accept the fact that you put your right hand on your hip, point your finger, or shake your head when you're talking down to someone (self-reflection). You must also face the fact you must stop using this body language (stop message). Once you're aware of the body language you use when you're being critical, say out loud or think to yourself. *I will remain calm, in discussing what I have to say* (Adult). Here is another example: *You've been told, and now accept the fact, that you roll your eyes when you're questioning someone's abilities at work* (self-reflection). Your self-talk could be this: *I'm in control of my facial expressions. I keep good eye contact with the person I'm speaking to* (recognition). *I've sent my Critical Parent out of the room* (visualization). *I use direct eye contact and portray concern and warmth as warranted* (Adult).

Practice self-control of your words and tone of voice. Knowing what words you use and how you sound will help you regulate. Again, if you aren't aware, ask a friend or a relative to give you details of your behavior.

Once you have an understanding about the volume of your voice and specific words you use, say out loud, or think to your self: *I control the tone of my voice and my words when having a conversation. If you raise your voice or name call, it's your Critical Parent who's trying to take control over the conversation.* This must stop if you want to be in control. You'll reinforce this control by saying out loud or using self-talk as follows: *I always take a moment to think through what it is I want to say, then, when I'm in control of my emotions, I address the issue in a calm manner and tone.*

Stop messages. It's vital that you stop your Critical Parent from sabotaging your conversations with people. I've given you several examples already on many of the stop messages you can use. Try some of the example stop messages or make-up your own. Make them simple and easy to remember.

Recall, after you use a stop message you must follow it up by a positive self-talk statement about the behavior you are trying to control. You must word your statement in positive terms. For example: *Stop rolling my eyes. I will keep my eyes directly on the person I'm speaking with.* Here's an example of wrong self-talk, *I **shouldn't** place my hands on my hip or shake my finger when I'm angry.* Your brain will associate quilt with placing your hands on your hips.

Visualization: Visualize whom your Critical Parent might look like. Don't let this surprise you if he/she looks like a familiar childhood memory. Don't be afraid to name him/her, it may help you when using stop messages. It's common for your Critical Parent to use the word "should" and remind you of mistakes. When this occurs, use a stop message and positive statement immediately.

Regulating your Critical Parent begins with accepting complete honesty. Once you accept these unique qualities about your "self", store them in your command center. The fact that you possess these characteristics are neither positive nor negative, it's how you choose to make the most of them that's important.

There will certainly be situations that warrant these qualities. However, this is the job for your Adult, your coach. You must trust yourself to be able to decide when to put your Critical Parent in the game. You may decide to bench your Critical Parent for an entire season. In some cases, this may not be a bad idea. (See diagram 7-3.)

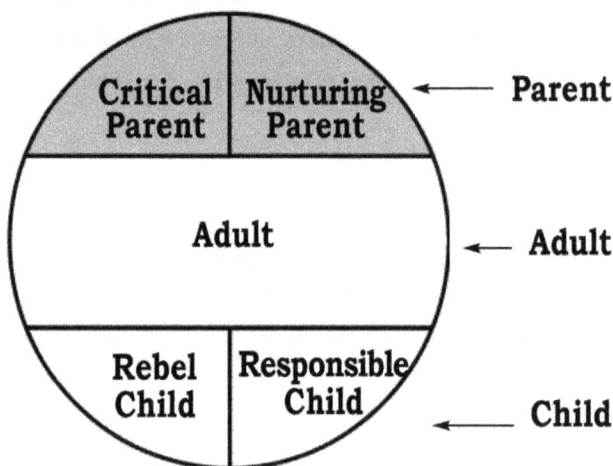

Diagram 7-3
The Critical Parent represents half of the total parent.

Adult

Self-Reflection: Please complete the exercise in chapter six. This exercise will help you know when, how, and what to say to maintain an adult point-of-view. In other words, to keep thoughts from spiraling out of control, you must maintain a positive, mature outlook and sense of composure.

Adult Self-Talk: The self-talk from this particular character is the **key tool** for gaining control of the remaining characters. In order to maintain emotional balance, it's imperative your self-talk be confident, logical, and rational. Think of this internal voice as the coach encouraging you to put your best foot forward to win! Winning in this case means resolving problems using business skills to seek a win-win scenario.

Say out loud or think to yourself: *I am in control. I solve problems resulting in a win-win solution. I handle problems in a rational and logical manner.*

Emotion Regulation: Express your feelings using your Adult. Practice Adult gestures. For instance, think about what and how you want to verbalize your feelings prior to confronting any one. Here is an example, say out loud or think: *At today's work meeting I'll show I have an open mind to employee's suggestions. I'll write down their ideas, paraphrase in my own words what each has to say, and clarifying if there is confusion.* Once you demonstrate you have good listening skills then find the best solution. Another example would be: *The next time my wife says I don't do anything to help her around the house, I'll tell her how this makes me feel. Then, we'll discuss what exactly she needs help with on a daily basis.* Remember to focus the conversation on how to solve the problem so both parties feel satisfaction about the outcome.

Practice your Adult tone of voice and vocabulary, then say out loud or use self-talk, as in the following example: *This weekend when my teenage son wants to borrow the car again, I'll listen attentively to his feelings. Then we'll discuss a plan of how he can help pay for insurance.* Use your Adult to help you negotiate ways in which both parties have a chance to come up with ideas of how to resolve the problem.

Stop messages: Use stop messages to help you with internal conflict. This occurs when you have two or more character's voices in your head. For example, if you have the Critical Parent speaking, the voice will be critical and pessimistic. Add the Nurturing Parent to the conversation to hear another voice that is kind and compassionate. Include the Adult to the dialogue and you'll hear a rational and logic voice.

Internal conflict occurs when you have two or more differences of opinion going on in your thoughts. People often refer to this internal battle as feeling overwhelming. Internal conflict is not negative as long as you permit your Adult to do its job, which is to hear the opinions of each character. Once you hear their opinions, use your reasoning abilities to come up with a solution that will get you the best results.

What do you do with this overwhelming feeling? Use stop messages to remind your self to slow down or STOP! Then, put your Adult into the driver's seat to drive your bus (positive self-talk statement). Remember, your Adult is the coach whose job is to manage the remaining team players. A coach's job is to direct decision-making, financial planning, maintaining and establishing relationships. Relying on your Adult will make you feel more in control of your life. (See diagram 7-4.)

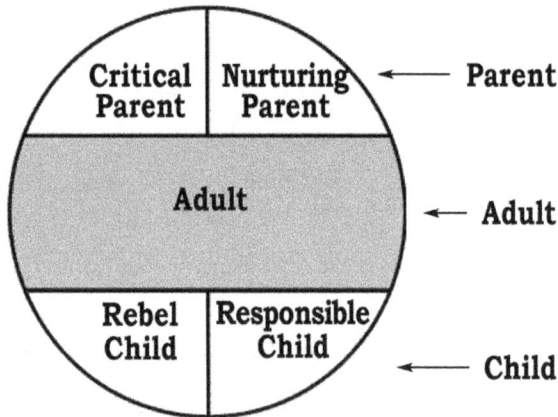

Diagram 7-4
The Adult is most qualified to drive your bus

Responsible Child
Self-Reflection: Please take a few minutes to complete the exercise in chapter six. Once you can recognize when your Responsible Child is *driving your bus,* you'll be able to regulate him or her appropriately.

Adult Self-Talk: Rely on your Adult self-talk to help express your Responsible Child's emotions. Say or think: *I express my feelings* (emotions) *about a problem* *in a calm, reasonable manner.* This type of self-talk will help you emotionally detach so you can communicate effectively.

Emotion Regulation: If you emotionally react to the problem or act out your feelings, it's your Responsible Child who is driving your bus. You are no longer thinking like an Adult, you are reacting emotionally like a child. Remember, a child does not have the necessary skills to figure out adult problems, so you cannot expect your Responsible Child to be any different.

Practice self-control of your child-like gestures. If you can recognize how you behave when you're feeling overly emotional, this will help you stay in control when your child is driving your bus. If you're not sure, ask someone you trust to show or explain how you behave. Again, you must have an open mind, smile, and thank them for their honesty.

You may realize some cute child-like behaviors about yourself, such as discovering you twist your hair when you're nervous, turning timid when around strangers, or telling jokes to get attention. Use self-talk to remind your "self'" not to scratch your ears, twist your hair, or rock back and forth during important meetings. For example, regulate your emotions by saying or thinking: *I'll be happy if I get a pay raise this year, but I'll be calm if it doesn't happen. If my coworkers get a raise, I'll be happy for them. I'll stay in control and reevaluate my options.* Another example of regulating your emotions with self-talk would be: *I'll give my class speech today with a calm voice, ease, and a sense of confidence.*

Again, practice self-control of your words and tone of voice. Knowing what you say and how it sounds will help you regulate your emotions. This is especially important when having disagreements in a relationship. It's easy to solve problems if each person recognizes when his or her emotions get out of control. If this occurs, use your Adult to get in control of your emotions. This will mean someone will have to wave the white flag and say, "I'm sorry for saying that. Let's take a deep breath and talk about it."

Stop message: Emotions are powerful and difficult to gain control of. That's why it's imperative that you use a stop message along with a positive self-talk statement, to help control these emotions of your child character. For example, *Stop sulking. I'm in control of my financial problems. I'll make an appointment tomorrow with a debt consolidator.*

Visualization: Imagine that your Adult is speaking on behalf of your child. This will protect your child from getting its feelings hurt. When you allow your child to speak for itself, you risk the chance of not getting the respect you deserve. For example, your boss continues to pile work on your desk. Instead of talking to your boss about her expectations, you sit at your desk and cry. Your boss asks you what's wrong. You say nothing and continue to cry. Your boss shakes her head questioning your professionalism.

Regulating your Responsible Child begins and ends with emotional control. It's the job of your Adult to help your child express its feelings appropriately. The fact you have an array of emotions is positive—it means you're alive and you know it! How you choose to express your emotions will determine how people will respect your feelings.

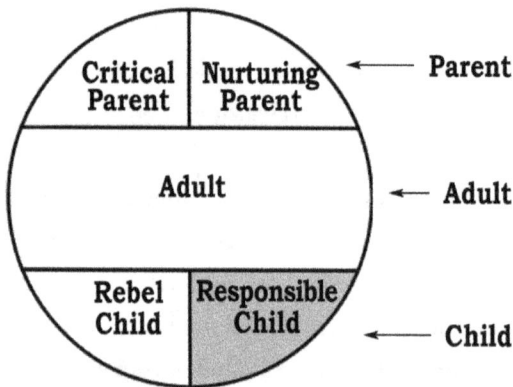

Diagram 7-5
The Responsible Child represents half of the total child.

Rebel Child

Self-Reflection: If you did not complete the exercise in chapter six, please take a few minutes to do so. Knowing how to use your aggression and passion to get positive results in life is the key to success. However, before you can see these results you'll need to learn how to regulate your rebellious "self." It's important you know your characteristics well. Self-reflection is the best way to get to know your rebellious "self."

Adult Self-Talk: Your self-talk will have to be firm but gentle. Remember, the goal of your rebellious child is to gain power. Your Adult cannot back down from your Rebel Child who is stubborn, revengeful, and arrogant. You're job is to reason with your Rebel Child who will challenge you and refuse to accept "No" for an answer. Your Adult must contend with this determination and persistence. Regulating your Rebel Child is like taming a wild horse. A wild horse will not accept being told what, how, or when to do things. A wild horse will not give up control. Your self-talk might sound like this: *I will stay in control when I have the urge to take risks.*

Emotion Regulation: Being able to express the emotions of your rebellious self will be challenging. Emotions range from anger to revenge to aggression. The goal is to be able to use your Adult to help you express these feelings in a manner that is socially acceptable. Taming a wild horse takes patience from your Nurturing Parent and Adult. For example, you know you have a tendency to be stubborn around Bill. He makes you so angry at times. Your self-talk would be: *I'm going to be receptive and respectful to Bill at all times.*

Another example, you know you're often aggressive with your teenage son, Chris, when he has problems in school. Use self-talk to reinforce the following: *This afternoon when I pick Chris up after school, I'll ask him if he wants to go have a pizza, just the two of us. During dinner we'll discuss what's important in his life, his friends, and his future plans.*

"Who are we protecting? Them or us?

Stop messages: In regulating your Rebel Child there is no place for your Critical Parent. Do not criticize your "self", as this will only lead to procrastination, low self-esteem, negative programming, and self-hatred. You can use stop messages and positive self-talk statements to remind your rebellious self to do the following: *Stop, I am calm. Stop, I always take a moment to think before I speak. Or, Stop, I'm sensitive to other's feelings.*

Visualization: Because it's power your Rebel Child is trying to display, picture yourself being rebellious. What are you wearing? What are your facial expressions and body language? Are you using drugs, alcohol, or smoking a cigarette? What type of music are you listening too?

Now, imagine yourself as an Adult. What are you wearing? What are your facial expressions and body language? What are you doing?

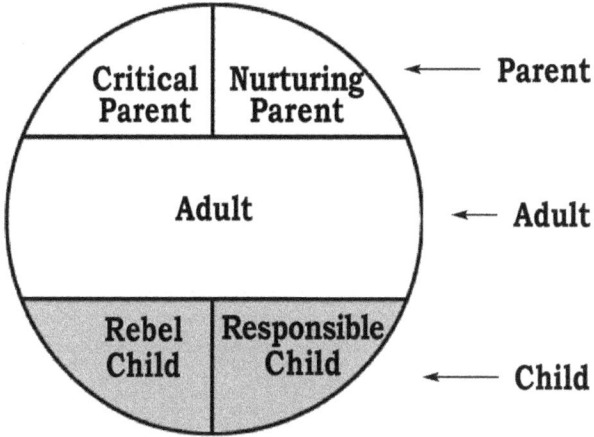

Diagram 7-6
The Rebel Child represents half of the total child.

– CHAPTER VIII –

REPLACE

Ego Bit: *The behavior we use is the behavior we choose.*

Now that you know how to regulate your five distinct characters, this chapter will explain when and how to replace one character for another, using real-life examples.

For instance, your sixteen-year-old son has come home late. What character can you use to effectively communicate your concerns? Remember, you have five characters to choose from, Critical Parent, Nurturing Parent, Adult, Responsible Child and Rebel Child. Let's assume you inadvertently select your Critical Parent. You begin to lecture and/or put-down your son. Then, suddenly you realize your son's body language is becoming defensive as he's starting to talk back to you. Please realize that when someone's rebellious side is showing this is your cue that things will soon be getting out of control. What should you do? It's time to replace your Critical Parent with another character, preferably your Adult.

How do I replace one ego for another?

Step 1. Recognize which particular character is driving your bus. In the above example, it's the Critical Parent.

Step 2. Regulate by using tools in chapter seven.

• **Use Adult self-talk.** Tell your Critical Parent to give up this power struggle with your teenage son. (Note: If you continue to use your Critical Parent to communicate with your son, you'll fuel his Rebel Child against you.)

• Control your emotions. Use stop messages to tell yourself to calm down so you can begin to think rational. Take a ten-minute break away from your son to get your thoughts together.

• Visualize yourself speaking to your son as though he were an employee or friend you respect.

• Eliminate negative body language such as finger pointing or hands on hips.

• Change your tone of voice and the expressions you use. Use a non-emotional (monotone) voice and respectful words when speaking.

Step 3. Replace your Critical Parent character with your Adult. It's your Adult who is responsible for appropriately handling problems and coming up with solutions.

With your Adult driving your bus, you'll achieve positive results using respect, logic, and rational thinking. In other words, think about how you'd discipline an employee if he/she were late for work. Some of you might say, "I'd fire him/her." However, you can't fire your children, but you can discipline them.

Here are some Adult ways of handling the situation: Dock their allowance or fine them by taking away privileges or time with friends. As a consequence, agree to use probation. Meaning, give them one warning before you enforce an agreed upon punishment. You could assign them extra work to make up for time lost. Teens will respond better if you ask them to come up with ideas for consequences. If you handle your family's problems more like a business, you'll be more apt to get positive results.

Here's another example to help you recognize when to replace your current character with a more suitable one.

Bill's Adult labors over the legal document he's composing. He allows his gaze to wander through the window of his office and settles on his coworker, Mary. She's talking on the phone and there's no doubt she's upset. He wishes he didn't notice a tear rolling down her cheek as she slams the phone down. Bill can't help but shake his head in sympathy for her and the problems she's having with her ex-husband. Getting up from his desk, he casually makes his way to her desk.

Bill gently places his palm on Mary's shoulder as he drops a small bag of jellybeans on her desk. "I hope everything's all right," he says in a soft tone. "If you need someone to talk to, I'm right here."

From this short example you can see how making the choice to replace the Adult for the Nurturing Parent benefits both Mary and Bill. This transformation occurs by paying particular attention to the differences in characteristics, which includes behavior, gesture, tone of voice, and vocabulary.

CHAPTER IX

RE-INVENT YOUR SELF

Developing Your Nurturing Parent -

Ego Bit: *If you expect someone to nurture you, you must first nurture yourself.*

What can you do if you feel you don't have the necessary nurturing tools? The key to developing your Nurturing Parent is to hone in and practice what you know or have seen from past or present experiences. Most of the knowledge you need is saved in your memory. It's a matter of taking time to do a self assessment. Say to yourself, *I know I have the skills to handle this situation. I just need a few minutes to gather my thoughts.*

After a self-assessment, you may decide you'd like to acquire additional tools to carry around. If so, begin by people watching. Go where people gather. Observe only nurturing behaviors, notice the little nuances and practice them.

For example, practice saying (or thinking), *This evening, when my teenage son is working on his computer, I'll pat him on a back. I'll tell him he's a good kid and that I'm proud of him.* Another example of self-talk to encourage your nurturing behavior would be: *Monday morning I'm going to give each of my employees a warm smile and ask how their weekend went.*

Other ways of acquiring nurturing skills is to adopt an elderly person in a retirement home, or volunteer as a mentor to work with disable children in your community. Volunteering to help others is the best way to develop additional nurturing skills. Practice what you learn with family and friends.

It's important to go one step further and nurture yourself through positive reinforcements. Pat yourself on the back and say, *I'm proud of myself for helping my neighbors in their time of need.* Or, *It makes me feel good knowing I've made a difference in someone's life today.* In learning new behavior you must be willing to repeat it. However, to repeat the behavior, you must receive positive reinforcement. This is the simplest way to change behavior.

So, who's driving your bus when a situation arises that needs you to be compassionate, empathic, and caring? Your Nurturing Parent is the most qualified to drive your bus when a person needs a helping hand, a shoulder to cry on, or a sympathetic ear. Reach into your toolbox and select a nurturing tool to gently handle the situation.

It's your Nurturing Parent who plays a significant role in bonding with others. Consequently, if you have a partner and/or are a parent, it's especially vital to have the ability to nurture your spouse and/or offspring. Having a well-developed Nurturing Parent is the foundation for a successful relationship and for effective parenting.

If you are experiencing moderate to severe problems in your intimate relationships and parenting, your Nurturing Parent may need to develop further. You may be having problems putting the needs of others before yours, for example, ignoring your child's need to spend one to one time with them. It may be difficult for you to cuddle or hug another person. You may avoid being around children, needy or ill people just so you don't have to deal with them. You may think volunteering is a waste of your time and charities are a rip off. You may avoid relationships all together because they take up so much of your personal time. You'd rather be working and making money, instead of lying on the beach making sand castles. Others may see you as a snob or too busy to hang out with.

Scenario:

Marcus glanced at Tim. Remembering to reach way down for a nurturing tool, he pulled out empathy and compassion and then commented, "Boy, you've really had a bad day at the office, haven't you?"

"You could say that."

Marcus didn't miss the frustrated edge to Tim's voice. Again, he decided to use his Nurturing Parent, Marcus asks, "Need a break? I sure do. Let's go have a cup of coffee."

"I could go for that."

The silence that followed them to the coffee room bothered Marcus, since Tim usually talked non-stop. Sitting at the table, coffee in hand, Marcus glanced at his employee. "Is everything all right?"

"If something could go wrong, believe me, it has."

"What's going on?" Marcus asked. (His Nurturing Parent is now in the driver's seat.)

"The twin boys got a touch of the flu yesterday and I was up all night taking care of them. You know my wife, Donna, has been suffering this past week with severe backaches from her C-section when delivering Anne. I'm beside myself trying to figure out how Donna is going to take care of a baby and the twins. She can barely get out of bed."

"I had no idea things were so demanding at home. You should have come to me, Tim. I remember when my wife and I had three little ones at home. It can be overwhelming. Go home, Tim. You have two weeks of sick leave that you've never taken. Go home and take care of your family."

"Thank you, Marcus. You have no idea how much this means to me and my family."

"See you in two weeks," Marcus repeated. "If that isn't enough time, call me and we'll work something out. Promise me, Tim?"

"Yes sir. And thank you."

Developing Your Critical Parent –

Ego Bit: *A person who has a critical eye also has an awareness of the world.*

What can you do to acquire tools necessary to set strict boundaries, remind others, and say "No"? You must develop them. First, realize it's essential to know how not to allow others to take advantage of you. This will help you live an emotionally well-balance life. Developing some of these characteristics is not negative when you use them from an Adult perspective.

The key to developing your Critical Parent is to first acknowledge these qualities as positive attributes. These traits are in your memory. Be aware that most people shy away from using these qualities due to associating them with negative or abusive memories. Others fear they may not know how to control these behaviors once they let them out.

To figure out which qualities you do have. Accomplish a self-assessment. Say to yourself: *I will choose characteristics and behaviors that are beneficial to others and me, and use them in a positive manner. I will critique, remind, and say "No" in a respectful way. I will allow my Adult to speak for me in the same manner I'd like to be spoken to under reverse conditions.*

Once you figure out which characteristics and behaviors are helpful, practice utilizing these skills in everyday situations. In the case of taking care of a pouting six-year-old child, your self-talk might sound like this: *When Sarah starts pouting at bed time, I'm going to listen attentively to her side of the story. Then, I'm going to validate what she says by telling her in my own words what I hear (nurturing). I'll speak to her in a calm, unemotional manner, remain open, and try to compromise if possible. I'll ask probing questions to find out exactly the reason for her discomfort. Is she afraid, hungry, or lonely? I'll seek the facts to solve the problem. Once I gather as much information as possible, I'll seek a "win-win" solution, so Sarah gets what she wants and I get what I want (Adult). However, I'll be ready to stick to my guns and say "No" if I feel her request is unreasonable or manipulative (critical).* Notice the majority of self-talk was on behalf of the Adult, Nurturing Parent and a few brief words from the Critical Parent.

Here is another example of how to practice these important traits. You are in a car accident, no one is hurt, but the driver of the other car is hysterical. You take control over the situation and direct the driver to, "Stop screaming, sit down, and relax! You're not hurt, and neither am I." Yes, you may come across as abrupt and bossy.

There will be times your Critical Parent will qualify to drive your bus. Usually this behavior is acceptable in times of emergency requiring quick action. These characteristics are an essential part of the overall Critical Parent character, especially for protection and warning.

"Lady, stop crying, you're fine! Calm down and call 911!"

Remember to pat yourself on the back when you're able to utilize these characteristics in a positive manner. *Say, I'm proud of myself for enforcing the house rules with my teenage son, without disrespecting him.* You can get people to do what you want them to do. It's just a matter of how people receive your message.

So, who's driving your bus when a situation arises that needs you to be firm, direct, and particular? Your Critical Parent can qualify to drive your bus when there are situations that require immediate attention to detail, emergency, and warning of danger or in military combat. This character is often known as the drill sergeant, because of its similar characteristics and behaviors. Regardless of whether or not you may hurt someone's feelings, there will be times you'll have to reach down into your toolbox to select a critical tool to give to your Adult to get the job done.

It's your Critical Parent who plays a major part in setting boundaries and enforcing rules. People who work in law enforcement, the military, medical emergency, and fire and rescue depend on their Critical Parent. Therefore, if you have a partner and/or are a parent, it's imperative to have the ability to warn, protect, and set boundaries.

If you are experiencing moderate to severe problems in your relationships, parenting, and work related issues, your Critical Parent may need to develop further. You may have problems in relationships because you are being the victim of abuse and don't know how to get out this situation. Your children may have run of the household because you fear they will not love you if you set rules. You feel people at work take advantage of you, because it's difficult to for you to say, "No." You settle for less, because you feel there's nothing you can do to control the situation. Others pity and feel sorry for you. This only keeps you in the victim mode. You are afraid to tell people how you really feel for fear of rejection.

This next scenario is an example of what could happen if you over use your Critical Parent.

Scenario:

Every Friday night, Martha headed across the street to unwind and share the workweek at the Café with Sue. It didn't take her long to spot her best friend.

"Hi! Sorry I'm late, had one of those Fridays!" Martha slid into the booth across from Sue and noticed her friend ordered a beer, instead of a soda.

"You must have had quite the week too, huh?"

"It's been more than trying. There's a new guy on my floor, Tom Johnson, and he thinks he's God's gift to women. Guess who he's hitting on?"

"You, because you're probably bringing it on yourself. Look how you're dressed today. You look like you're going out on the town instead of work. And, as usual

your perfume is too strong. You shouldn't wea
of those see-through-bras." Martha motioned

"I can't believe you!"

"What? I'm just telling you the truth, you
wouldn't want me to lie, would you?" Sue
seemed surprised… and ticked.

"I merely said 'Hello' to Tom. You think
I'm encouraging him to flirt with me?"

"No, I'm merely saying your short skirts
and tight tops say you're available to men."

"That's ridiculous."

Martha breathed deep, as she leaned against the booth. "Did I not remind
you over and over not to date men at work? I don't mean to sound like your
mother, but your hair color needs to be toned down, too." It suddenly occurred
to Martha that Sue had grown quiet. Martha noticed a single tear stream down
her friend's face, followed by a wet stream of others. Martha stopped talking and
watched her friend wipe at her tears.

"Sue, I'm so sorry. I don't know what got into me. Did I say those things to you?
I can't believe my own ears. I… my aunt use to talk to me like that… about the
guys who use to come around the house. I use to hate when she would talk to
me like that. Now look at me. I sound just like her. Please, forgive me?"

Developing Your Adult –

Ego Bit: *Responsibilities are the rewards we obtain in adulthood.*

*"Let's brainstorm together how we can solve this
problem you're having in school. Any ideas son?"*

What can you do to obtain the tools you need to help you think rational, logical, and solve problems? The key to developing your Adult is to take the initiative to educate yourself. Begin by observing a role model you respect. Ask questions. Attend management seminars or take human development classes to educate yourself on human behavior. Watch educational videos on The Learning Channel. Seek professional guidance from a counselor or psychologist. Ask for or take on more responsibilities at home or at work.

Most importantly, rely on what you already know. Once you learn a new skill, put it into practice. If it doesn't work, try another one, then another, until you find one that does work for you.

Practice using your business skills to help you maneuver through all personal and professional situations. What do I consider as business skills? Skills you already use to manage finances, attend school or work, and maintain relationships. It's being a productive and responsible person in society. Without business skills you'll have a difficult time functioning in society.

Recall, the Adult is the foundation for professional and personal relationships. It's through the method of Adult self talk that will transform you into a responsible, common sense, and law-abiding person. Being an Adult means taking responsibility for where you are in life and the problems you create. If you're not communicating effectively with your children or partner—learn a different way. Put your Adult in the driver's seat and stop complaining.

Recall in chapter two, Johnny's mother replaces her Critical Parent for her Nurturing Parent at the grocery store. After Johnny's nap, his mother tells him he'll be going to a doctor's appointment with her. On the way they stop for gas, she replaces her Nurturing Parent for her Adult to speak to Mike, an old classmate from High School. Johnny's mother remains an Adult while she waits for her appointment at the doctor's office. Upon their departure, she replaces her Adult for her Nurturing Parent to compliment Johnny for his Adult behavior.

Here's a scenario where you'd like to talk to your partner about the fact she's spending too much money on buying shoes. Your Adult self-talk might sound like this: *I'm going to ask Janice out to dinner* (family meeting) *to discuss some financial issues. While at dinner, I'll ask her opinion on how she can continue to buy what she enjoys and still save for a down payment on the new house* (win-win solution). *I'll keep the conversation upbeat and keep an open mind to her suggestions* (brain storming). *I won't bring up her shoe purchasing. In fact, I'll take notice of her new pair and how nice they look on her feet* (nurturing). Notice this self-talk is mainly from the Adult and Nurturing Parent perspective each voicing their opinions.

What would internal conflict sound like? With reference to the partner who spends too much on footwear, it might sound like this. Enter the Critical Parent:

That's it! I'm setting down some strict rules for using the credit card. I'll remind her who's the breadwinner. Every week she stuffs another pair of my hard-earned cash in her closet!

Enter the Rebel Child: *Dinner! Forget it! As soon as I get home, I'm going to tell her that I'm quitting my job and she can support the family. We'll see if she continues to spend money on stupid stuff. Maybe then she'll appreciate the long hours I put in at work.*

Enter the Nurturing Parent: *I can't talk to her like that, how rude. I can't demand she get a job, what about the baby? She's a fantastic mother and cook. I don't want some stranger raising our kids. She's perfectly happy working at home. I don't know how she does it? It's the toughest job anyone can have. I know I couldn't do it. Janice loves being a mother and wife. She never complains about anything. I need to be more compassionate to her needs.*

Enter the Adult: *I need to calm down, it's not like she's buying expensive shoes. She's awesome at budgeting and finding bargains. She's earning each pair of shoes and deserves a million pairs of shoes for all she's done for the kids and me. The real problem is how do we cut back further on expenses so we can save money for a down payment on a new house? I'll use patience and understanding with Janice. I'll just talk with her over dinner and voice my concerns, so we can decide what to do together.*

Enter the Responsible Child: *I wish I didn't have to work so many hours. I just want to lie out on the beach and have fun. Some days I daydream about living at home with mom and dad again. I didn't have a worry in the world. I wish someone would take care of me.*

Note: This dialogue between characters can go on for days if you allow it to. If it does, this is an example of feeling overwhelmed to the point of obsessing.

Don't forget to give yourself credit for getting your Adult in the driver's seat. Say to yourself: This situation could have easily turned into a shouting match, but I remained calm and rational. I did a fantastic job!

So, who's driving your bus when it comes to rational thinking and problem solving? Your Adult qualifies to drive your bus when decisions need to be made, problems need to be solved, and financial and legal issues need to be addressed. When in doubt, reach into your toolbox to choose an adult tool to help resolve the problem.

If you are experiencing moderate to severe problems in your personal and professional relationships, work, and legal and financial problems, your Adult may need to develop further. For example, others may think of you as irresponsible and too much of a kid. You'd rather let someone else take the lead in personal and professional relationships. You may purposefully sabotage job promotions that would yield you more responsibility. You secretly wish you were still a kid living at home with mom and dad. You seek out partners who you know love kids, so they'll take good care of you. You're so emotional people tease you about it. You hate going to work. Bill collectors are calling you because you forget to pay bills. You let someone else handle all your business dealings. You feel like a big kid in an Adult's body. The best time of the day is when you get to play.

Scenario:

Mrs. Garcia sat in the kitchen drinking tea as she waited for her sixteen-year-old daughter to come home from the movies. She watched her daughter inch the door open and tiptoe inside. "No use sneaking in, I'm sitting up waiting for you. Did you have a good time?"

"Sure did, Mom. Sorry I'm late again." Cindy said with an apologetic tone. "I suppose you're really mad at me, aren't you?"

Mrs. Garcia paused before she said what really was on her mind. She took a deep breath, remembered to treat this matter from an Adult perspective—use no emotion. "Cindy, I'm not mad, my concern is we're not communicating like we use to. Do you have any suggestions on how we can fix this problem?" She watched her daughter's expression change from surprised to serious.

"I know you and Dad want me home at nine o'clock on school nights. I know the rules. It's just that Trent puts pressure on me to stay out late with him," confessed Cindy.

"How does that make you feel?"

"I feel torn between the people I love and care about."

"So the problem you're having is how do you obey the house rules to please me and your father, while trying to please your boyfriend? Is that right?"

"That's exactly right, Mom. I've been stressing out about it."

"Well, Cindy, now that we know what the problem is, let's come up with some ideas on how to solve it. Let's have a cup of hot chocolate and see if we can figure out a way you can follow the house rules and still not upset your boyfriend."

"Maybe Trent could come over here and watch TV or work on the computer with me after nine?"

"You'd be home and be able to spend a little more time with Trent. I could see that working. He'd have to leave by ten, though, " Mrs. Garcia compromised.

"That's cool, he has to be home by ten-thirty anyway.

Gee, thanks, Mom. I'm sleepy now. Can I go to bed?"

"Sure Honey."

*"So, you feel pressure by your boyfriend to disobey our rules?
Let's see if we can come up with some ideas together."*

Developing Your Responsible Child –

Ego Bit: *Are you feeling stressed? If so, take time to laugh and play.*

What can you do if you feel you can't seem to relax or have fun? The key to developing your Responsible Child is to explore your inner child. This means take a moment to remember the most positive moments in your childhood such as a birthday party, playing with your best pal or pet, and eating mud pies. Think back to your feelings of puppy love as you made "goo-goo" eyes at the Responsible Child of another. As love blossoms, it's your Adult that verbalizes a commitment (a contract) for a monogamous relationship.

Remember as a youngster how you would laugh, sing, and play? These are the same qualities you need to incorporate in your daily life to feel emotional balance. These traits are deep within. Every person has pleasant memories of their childhood. It's a matter of remembering those times.

Most people tend to use less and less of their child character as they take on more Adult responsibilities such as marriage, raising children, and work. Ironically, we're in such a hurry to grow up we ignore or forget how to use our kid. Then again, there are those who refuse to grow up and overuse their child.

When you express emotional feelings such as sadness, fear, joy, or loneliness, it's the tears of your child character that are rolling down your face. You may experience sensations of feeling particularly young or may behave in a child-like manner.

What if you just can't remember any positive memories of your childhood? Ask a childhood friend, relative, or neighbor to help you remember the fun and silly things you said or did, such as play sports, tell jokes, fly kites, and build sand castles.

For those of you whose childhood was cut short due to parents who were ill, parents who had drug or alcohol problems, or parents who were abusive. Your journey in getting to know your inner child begins with learning to trust yourself and others. This means you must learn to nurture your child by taking him or her out for a good time. For example if you've had the desire to paint, buy yourself an easel—go for it. If you love to sing or want to learn to play an instrument just do it. Age is not an issue.

Ask your Nurturing Parent to gently take your child by the hand to encourage emotional growth, just as you would your own child. Ask your Adult to pick up the phone and gather pertinent information from the YMCA, community college, golf course, or craft store on activities that interest you.

Find a role model to help you begin. Call your best friend or invite a co-worker to join you. You may get a surprise at how many of your friends would love to try something new. It's a matter of taking the first step. You'll find the next step is even easier. Developing your child means looking at life through a child's view with enthusiasm and curiosity.

So, who's driving your bus when it comes to showing and expressing emotions? Your Responsible Child qualifies to drive your bus to help your Adult express these emotions in a sincere manner. All you have to do is reach into your toolbox to pull out any positive emotion you remember experiencing as a child. Then, use your Adult to help communicate your feelings. It's this validation of your feelings that will help you feel love and respect. If you rely on your child to communicate feelings, you'll come across as immature, too emotional or overwhelming. I'm not saying you can't cry. I'm saying you need your Adult to speak on behalf of your crying child. Having balance in your Responsible Child is crucial to having balance in your "self" to successfully express your feelings.

If you are experiencing moderate to severe problems with having fun, laughing, and relaxing, your Responsible Child may need to develop further. Others may think of you as no fun or annoying. You may experience problems expressing feelings, lack meaningful relationships, and have few friends or interests. You avoid joining sports teams or organized clubs where you know you may have fun. You turn down party invitations because you don't know how to have fun with others. You get irritated when people are laughing around you because you are paranoid they may be laughing at you. You think people who have fun are wasting their time and should be working. You have difficulties acting like a kid around your children.

If you grew up in an environment with a Critical Parent, you may lack self-confidence, fear rejection, or be untrusting. This may help explain why you come across to others as no fun, shy or a loner.

Scenario:

Andy loves his job as sales representative for a computer-consulting firm. His favorite time of day is the mid afternoon coffee break, which happens to be right now. Reaching for the phone, he dials his boss. "Hey, Tony, I'll bet you lunch tomorrow that my Hummer's faster than your race car. What do you say?"

"In your dreams, buddy. This time I'm picking the restaurant, the last place you picked was disgusting!"

Andy laughed, and answered, "You're on. Meet you at the starting line." Andy reached under his desk and grabbed a battered, red, remote Hummer truck, a birthday gift years ago from his fiancée. He hurried down the hallway and placed his truck next to Tony's fancy, fifty-seven Chevy convertible.

"Something happen to Ruby, that piece of junk looks rather ratty?" Tony asked, fake sarcasm lacing his words.

"You're just jealous of my Ruby. There's no way you're going to beat me today. Ruby Red-Dress is equipped with new batteries!" Andy laughed, as he snapped a new hat on his head. He nodded at his secretary as she held her hand-made checker flag for this important event. "Margie, I think we're ready."

"On your mark! Gentlemen start your engines! Go!" Margie screamed, then burst into laughter.

The once empty halls now surged with hopping and hollering people. As he expected, coworkers pointed, laughed and made silly remarks at Andy's new, bright yellow hat, in the shape of a banana. "Don't laugh, I need any edge to throw Tony off guard."

"I can't believe you'd stoop so low as to wear something as ugly as that," Tony said, in mocked shock. Once he started laughing at the spectacle Andy made, it seemed Tony couldn't stop. His Chevy smashed into the wall and darted across the hallway into the opposite wall. Because of his uncontrollable laughing, he struggled to keep his convertible moving down the hall.

Tony wiggled his head and made ape sounds, the crowd went wild with laughter. It didn't take Andy long to guide Ruby Red-Dress past the finish line. Margie crossed over the checkered flag, and he smiled and raised his arms triumphantly.

"We have a winner, again, it's Ruby Red-Dress taking first!"

" Go Ruby... go!"

"Okay, Andy, you're lucky this time, but there's always tomorrow. Besides, you cheated with that stupid hat," Tony said, shaking his head in mocked annoyance.

"It's pizza for lunch tomorrow. I'm already hungry," Andy said, picking up his old truck. "There's no comparison between that fancy new rig of yours and my faithful Ruby!" Andy smiled as the crowd applauded his comment.

The crowd dissipated as quickly as it had appeared. The time had come for the boss, Andy, and the employees, to return to the adult world of work. As Andy walked back to his office, he chuckled to himself and wondered how truly ridiculous he looked in his banana-shaped hat. He'll have to give some thought to what distraction he could create for tomorrow. This racing had bonded the entire office, and the laughter put them all in a good mood. He hadn't enjoyed working for a company more than this one. Andy smiled with that thought.

Developing Your Rebel Child -

Ego Bit: *Those who lack confidence have never overcome adversity.*

"Now slowly hand over the three percent pay raise you've been promising for two years, and I'll get back to work quietly."

What can you do to become more of a risk taker and more aggressive at times? The key to developing your Rebel Child is to choose wisely from your characteristics. You can use rebellious characteristic in a positive fashion to achieve positive results. However, if you use these characteristics you need to be aware there will be both positive and negative consequences.

Because these traits are vital in the survival of ones dignity, remember, it's how you choose to use these characteristics that count. Having an underdeveloped Rebel Child presents just as many problems as having an overdeveloped one. An underdeveloped character will be pushed around and restrained from taking chances. You'll accept second best and have self-hatred. To develop a healthy rebellious child doesn't mean you have to rob a bank or start picking fights with people. I'm simply saying if you take more risks in life in a well-thought out Adult manner, you'll achieve more goals and feel more in control of your life.

The consequences of taking risks may equal failure or rejection. However, this will help you grow a thicker, emotional skin. Risks can be situations such as introducing yourself to a person you want to meet. Quitting your safe and unchallenging job for a more exciting one that offers less pay or benefits. Going back to school to get that engineering or web designer degree. Or other risks like flying lessons, hiking Glacier National Park, or going on an African safari. In other words, don't take "No" for an answer when it comes to your abilities or life style. There is a certain amount of rebellious nature you must have in order to live life to it's fullest.

When is it appropriate to use my Rebel Child characteristics? There will be occasions when it's necessary to have your Rebel Child drive your bus. A case in point: for the protection of yourself and loved ones from harm. You may need to show aggression through body language, vocal tone and vocabulary, or physical force. An example of this would be disobeying authority, taking a risk in breaking the speed limit to rush your child to the emergency room in order to save his or her life.

Voicing your opinion in an assertive manner, with the help of your Adult, is important to get your point across or test boundaries. Children will tell a lie to protect themselves or siblings in abusive situations. Adults will tell half-truths to protect their reputation, jobs, or family (depending on the circumstances).

Use of alcohol: The use of alcohol for social or business situations is condoned when used sparingly. It's all in how you regulate your Rebel Child and how you use emotional control and self-talk from your Adult.

How can your use anger in a positive manner? First, remember anger is a normal feeling. It is an expression of your Rebel Child. Do not mistake it for a bad emotion. This emotion can motivate you toward positive changes in your life. The fact that your rebellious "self" may get angry and refuse to accept "No" does help in some situations. Examples of this would be, standing up for your self, not giving up, and having self motivation. It's your Rebel Child that takes risks in life just to prove the impossible can be done.

So, who is driving your bus when it comes to taking risks, challenging authority, and throwing temper tantrums? It's your Rebel Child who's vying for power and control. Due to the possible results of these characteristics, most people are afraid to use them. However, in order to have balance in your "self" there will be times you'll need to pull a trait or two out of your toolbox. It'll be up to your Adult to speak and act on behalf of your Rebel Child in a dignified, assertive manner. Having the skills to take risks in life is necessary in order for you to achieve your goals.

If you are experiencing moderate to severe problems such as being the victim in relationships or by strangers, your Rebel Child may need to develop further. In other words, you've been a prime target for people to beat up on. Others may pity or feel sorry for you. You may expect others to fight your fights, especially if you are the baby of the family. Having either an older sibling or a parent's protection as a youngster can handicap you in adulthood. To reverse this action, you must stop being the victim and develop a certain amount of warrior spirit to keep your "self" safe.

What happens to a person if you expose him or her to a continual Rebel Child environment? I'll answer the question by going back to our story about Johnny and his mother. If Johnny's mother continues to expose him to her aggressions and criticisms, chances are he too will develop an overbearing Rebel Child and

Critical Parent. There's a good chance he'll begin to have difficulties in school, with peers, and with authority figures.

If Johnny's exposure continues into his teen-age and young adulthood he'll be a high risk for employment problems, legal and financial problems. He'll probably develop drug and alcohol related problems. And Johnny will more than likely have several unstable and/or abusive relationships—physically, emotionally, or verbally.

Scenario:

Jason could hardly believe Marcia would agree to go to counseling with him. They've only been married for six months. Because he really loved Marcia, Jason was willing to try anything at this point to save their relationship. He couldn't understand why Marcia had such a terrible temper and needed help on how to handle it.

He thought back to last Friday night when he'd complained about her temper. She didn't like him nagging her about it. It had gotten to a point where she'd yell, scream, and even stomp her feet just like a child. That evening, Marcia actually pushed him down onto the couch and screamed profanities at him. She then threw their wedding photo to the floor. She had sounded and acted just like his Uncle Jake, and that worried Jason.

He walked into the counselor's office and discovered Marcia had already arrived. "You're here! I'm not too late, am I?" he asked, his voice tightened as he sat in the chair beside his new bride.

"Not at all. I'm Samuel Weber," the counselor said, extending his right hand toward Jason.

"Hi," he said, shaking the tall, thin man's hand.

"I've had a chance to chat with Marcia while we waited for you. She's done a great job filling me in as why you made this appointment. Let's get started by discussing what both your parents were like when you were growing up, Jason can we start with you?"

"From what I remember, my parents were extremely loving to me. They both died in a boating accident when I was ten years old. My father always made sure my mother and I had a life jacket on, but that particular day mom took hers off to sun bathe. I was the only survivor from the accident. I have an older sister, Jenny who was visiting my aunt and uncle that day. We were both adopted by them after the accident." Jason answered, wondering what the connection was.

"I'm sorry to hear about your parents. How did your aunt and uncle treat you in their care?"

"It was like a war zone." Jason answered, nearly laughing at his description. "Marriage in heaven it wasn't. Uncle Jake would nag Aunt Beth night and day about not keeping a decent house. Sometimes he'd just up and leave for days. When he did come home, he'd be drunk, harass my sister, and me and throw things around the house. He'd drive my Aunt Beth nuts."

"What do you think was going on with him? Did he have problems at work?"

"I guess he had a really good job when they first got married. He was a banker for about five years, made good money, too. I remember my parents talking about how successful Uncle Jake was, especially when he came by the house to take my dad for a ride in his new convertible Corvette. Then, I guess the recession hit his bank hard and he had to sell his car and move into an apartment. When I moved in, Uncle Jake worked two jobs, and my Aunt Beth took up sewing to earn some extra money. I think my aunt was so busy keeping up with her sewing jobs it was impossible for her to keep up with the housework, but he continued to nag her despite how busy Uncle Jake knew she was."

"Was he physically abusive to your aunt?"

"Heck no. He'd just drink and scream at her something fierce. I use to go to my room and put my earphones on, hoping to drown out his yelling. It didn't work that much. Uncle Jake would tell my Aunt Beth she was good-for-nothing and a slob."

"How did these comments make you feel? " the counselor asked.

"I feel bad for my Aunt Beth. No matter what she does, it isn't good enough. Even now, at fifty-five-years-old, he continues to yell at her for minor things, he drinks heavily, and he gives my step-brother a tough time."

"Marcia, do you nag Jason?"

"I guess I do. I never thought about it. It seems that if I don't remind him of things over and over again, he forgets them. I guess I do have a tendency to criticize and put Jason down. I don't mean to, but I guess I sort of treat him like a child. It's the way my mom got me to do things or remember stuff."

"How does that make you feel, Jason?"

"It ticks me off. Marcia sounds like my Uncle Jake. I don't want to live in a home like the one I grew up in. I don't feel like coming home sometimes. I don't' understand what I do that warrants her yelling at me like a bad little boy?"

"Do you understand what's happening here?" the counselor asked. "Marcia each time you remind or yell at Jason this triggers childhood memories of living at home with Uncle Jake. So, Jason you're reacting to Marcia as if you're living at home. You're rebelling by not doing things or by running off to your room. Using the Who's Driving Your Bus model, Marcia is using her Critical Parent, which will only elicit Jason's Rebel Child. So you both are fueling the fire, so to speak. It's important to realize both of your behaviors are learned behavioral patterns from your role models early in life."

"What can we do so we don't talk down or act rebellious towards each other?" Marcia asked.

"First, you must learn to recognize when you're being critical or rebellious. This will include recognizing how you behave, what vocabulary and tone of voice you use. Second, regulate this unnecessary behavior by using a method called, self-talk. Self-talk is what you say to yourself—it's your internal voice. Use your Adult, who is your rational and logical side, to help communicate for you. Next, once you realize you're using your Critical Parent or Rebel Child, replace the character with your Adult. Think about how you'd handle yourself in a business meeting if you had a disagreement with your boss or a co-worker. Who would you want to be driving your bus? Would you yell, use put-downs, or throw things around at work? I think you get my point. So who's driving your bus?" asked the counselor.

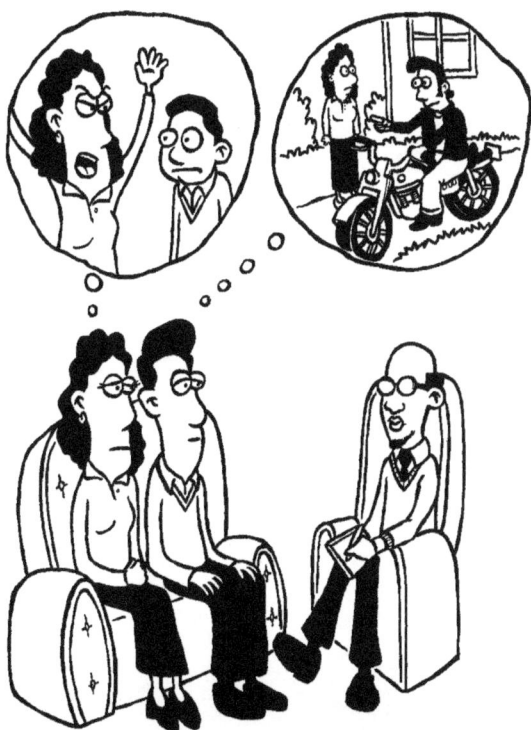

"So you are constantly reminding him to pick up his things and he's acting like a rebellious teenager?"

CHAPTER X

QUESTIONS & ANSWERS

Ego Bit: *You are what you think. Positive thoughts ripen into positive actions.*

I'm thirty-three years old and grew up in an abusive home. I did not receive any nurturing from my parents. How can I begin to develop my Nurturing Parent?

It's never too late to learn nurturing skills. First, take a moment to jot down your existing skills. By doing this, you'll discover that in-fact you do have skills. Then, buy yourself a small plant to care for and love. If you make it through the first six months without loosing your plant, graduate to a few more. Next, if you can have a pet, begin reading up on caring for a turtle, hamster or puppy. Then, make a trip to your local pet store or shelter to choose your new child.

Studies have shown that how you nurture your plants and pets is how you'll nurture others.

Other ways of acquiring nurturing skills is to adopt an elderly person in a retirement home, or volunteer as a mentor to work with disable children in your community. Volunteering to help others is the best way to develop additional nurturing skills. Then, practice what you learn with family and friends.

In addition, it's important to go one step further and nurture yourself through positive reinforcements. Pat yourself on the back and say, *I'm proud of myself for helping my neighbors in their time of need.* Or, *It makes me feel good knowing I've made a difference in someone's life today.* To develop a new behavior that is consistent to your personality you must be willing to repeat it.

I'm always taking care of people and their problems as if I'm the parent. Now I feel taken advantage of. What can I do?

Develop your Rebel Child so you can learn to say "No." People who are extremely nurturing have a difficult time rocking the boat. Inadvertently, you become the victim because you place everyone else's wants and needs before yours. While your wants and needs simmer slowly and quietly on the back burner (this is how you get burnt). It's impossible to take care of everyone. So, it's okay to say, "No. I'm sorry I don't know how to advise you on that." You're not responsible for fixing everyone's problems. Taking time for you is a way to develop your rebellious side—by being selfish.

Rebellious traits are vital in the survival of ones dignity, remember, it's how you choose to use these characteristics that count. Having an underdeveloped Rebel Child presents just as many problems as having an overdeveloped one. An underdeveloped character will be pushed around and restrained from taking chances. You'll accept second best and begin to have self-hatred.

To develop a healthy rebellious child doesn't mean you have to rob a bank or start picking fights with people. I'm simply saying you are not responsible for everyone's problems. You are not everyone's social worker. Take time for you, you'll achieve more goals and feel more in control of your life.

How do I avoid being too critical or manipulated by my children?

Avoid being critical and manipulated by using your Adult. Try to seek balance between both your Nurturing and Critical Parent. In other words, try not to be too much of a nurturer or too much of a critical parent. (See diagram 7-3.) If either your Critical or Nurturing Parent dominates your personality this is considered an unbalance in your "self." For example, if you're being more critical than nurturing chances are your children will perceive you as a nagging parent. (See diagram 10-1.)

However, if you rely on your Adult to help your Critical Parent set boundaries and enforce rules. You can get your children to do what you want them to do.

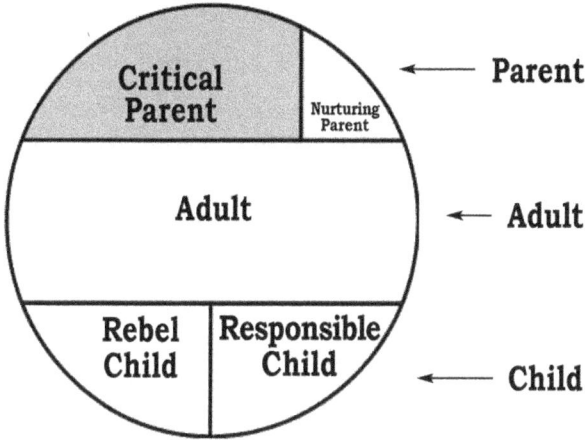

Diagram 10-1

It's just a matter of how they receive your message. In other words, if your child perceives you are using your Critical Parent to speak to them, they will pull out his or her Rebel Child to talk back. However, if you use your Adult to help relay your Critical Parent's concerns in a calm and rational conversation, your child will be more apt to respect you and pull out his or her Adult to compromise. Same thing applies with using your Nurturing Parent. If you are too nurturing with your child he or she may use this to their advantage to manipulate you. When you use your Nurturing Parent, your child will automatically bring out his or her Responsible Child. Though the Responsible Child is an overall good kid, you may not get the results you want. If you want to make your child responsible for his actions, stick to using your Adult. Using your Adult will bring out your child's (even though they may be under the age of ten). This is how your child will develop his or her Adult.

My children and wife complain that I'm too bossy. How can I stop this behavior?

First, begin by recognizing what your Critical Parent's characteristics are. Then be aware of your expressions and what circumstances bring out your critical characteristics. If you're having difficulties knowing when your Critical Parent is talking, ask your children or wife to kindly point out your behavior. Ask them to be specific as to physical behaviors, tone of voice, gestures, and vocabulary.

The Critical Parent usually drives your bus when you want to take control over people and things. You'll sense a lack of control prior to feeling like you need to take control. Your Critical Parent enjoys showing up without an invitation, which can be bad news for loved ones or any person who gets in his or her way. Practice using your Nurturing Parent to help you apologize for your impatient, bossy, and abrupt behavior. The more you use your Nurturing Parent this will offset the use of your Critical Parent. You'll begin to feel a sense of balance in your "self."

When all else fails—use your Adult to help you communicate effectively. Whenever you want to give guidance to your family members do so in a business-like manner. Treat all family problems on the same level of respect, just as you would solve a problem with a co-worker. Keep all the emotions out of the conversation and look for a win-win solution.

During office meetings, I have a tendency to be pushy and close my mind to suggestions. How can I be more diplomatic?

Make a conscious effort not to bring your critical "self" to work. Begin by having a clear picture of what your Critical Parent looks and sounds like. When you get up in the morning, leave your Critical Parent cleaning the house or garage. Take only your unemotional, rational, logical, and calm Adult to work. When you bring your Critical Parent to an office meeting expect to have the following attitude and self-talk: *Everyone is wrong; and I'm right! And I'm going to beat it down their throats until they see it my way.* Remember, if you hear this critical voice in your next office meeting, switch immediately to your positive Adult self-talk, which might sound like this: *I will have an open mind to other's opinions. I'll wait my turn to speak and then I'll respond in a considerate and professional manner.* Self-talk of this type will help you gain control over your critical self.

When away from the office educate your Adult "self" on subjects pertaining to effective communication, the art of negotiations and mediation. This information will teach you valuable techniques in finding a win-win solution.

How can your book help me be successful in business?

One way would be to learn to use your Adult effectively. In business your success or failure will depend on how well you communicate, which involves basic skills such as active listening, paraphrasing, and clarifying. These skills help in gathering facts, validating people's opinions, and relaying information. Business is about people and seeking win–win solutions. Problem solving is all about effective communication.

Another way, is to learn to seek balance between all four characters, with the exception of your Adult (see diagram 7-1). In business, there are a number of ways to benefit from your ability to be flexible. You may be the one co-worker's and supervisors rely on for rational and logical thinking. This may open the doors to promotions, responsibilities and increase in salary. People in business like to be around other people who a re compassionate, good communicators, confident, fun, daring and who can say "No." My book will help you regulate your characters by using the tools in chapter seven. If you want to re-invent your "self," make sure you study chapter nine.

My partner and I cannot disagree without it turning into an argument. What seems to be happening?

You need to have a sit down meeting with your partner to establish Adult ground rules for disagreements. Some suggestions for ground rules are; tone of voice needs to remain calm and unemotional. Gestures are to be open and encouraging. Another good ground rule is to stay in the here and now, which means don't bring up past problems. Make sure each of you gets equal time to voice your opinion and paraphrase. (Summarize to your partner in your own words what you heard from their perspective.) After you have established basic ground rules, then make a list of guidelines to follow, for example:

1. State the problem in as few words as possible.

2. Brainstorm several different ideas to remedy the problem.

3. Include a ten-minute time out, if either partner is getting emotional.

4. Select the best idea based on a win-win scenario.

Sign and post these guidelines on the fridge for future use.

What kind of personality does an over-developed Responsible Child have?

This individual would be a big kid in an adult's body. He or she probably would enjoy working in jobs such as music, sports, art, or theater. This individual probably seeks situations that would put them at the center of attention or alone to do what they want to do. This individual may come across as selfish or totally engross in what it is they do. Some may say more often than others, "Look at me! See what I can do!" In relationships, this individual may get restless with the same playmate and is eager to have many playmates. This individual usually seeks out partners whose personality leans toward the Nurturing Parent, so they will be taken care of.

At age thirty, is it too late to develop a healthy Responsible Child?

No. In fact, age has nothing to do with whether or not you can or cannot develop a healthy Responsible Child. Ask your inner child what his or her yearnings have been since childhood. You might want to take piano lessons, learn to play tennis, ride a horse, scuba dive, or act in a play. Whatever the case may be, take your Responsible Child by the hand and enroll him or her in classes. Then go for it and have a blast!

When I get angry with my coworkers and family, I throw a temper tantrum or use profanity. How can I get my point across without being aggressive?

Temper tantrums occur because you feel you don't have a voice or control over the situation. So it's easy to use your Rebel Child to help you gain power and control. If you throw a temper tantrum or use profanity, immediately apologize on behalf of your Rebel Child's behavior. It's okay to be upset, but it's not okay to over power someone to get your point across. Regulate your emotions by relying on your Adult to speak up for you. Use positive self-talk to rehearse in your mind, in a calm, rational manner, what, how, and when you'll say what you have to say. The key is to learn to communicate in an Adult manner, not in an uncontrollable, regretful manner.

Explain, using your methodology, why domestic violence occurs.

Domestic violence occurs when one party's Rebel Child beats up on the other party's Responsible Child. For example: a bully beating up on a kid on the playground. Extreme violence occurs when both parties insist on using their rebellious behaviors to hurt each other. This can result in verbal, emotional, or physical attacks on each other, which can lead to death. It's as if two angry kids are throwing rocks and screaming profanity on the playground.

CHAPTER XI

PEOPLE WHO COMMIT CRIMES

Ego Bit: *The less power your have the more you like to use it.*

"You're going to end up just like your father... an alcoholic and in prison."

Who's driving the bus of individual's who commit crimes?

The Rebel Child and Critical Parent are the characters in the driver's seat.

Are these individual unstable?

Yes. They are unstable in the sense their characters are not in balance of one another. It's due to having a dominant Rebel Child and Critical Parent. An individual with a dominant Rebel Child and Critical Parent will have an underdeveloped Adult and Nurturing Parent. Unless the offender's is willing to develop his or her Adult and Nurturing Parent, they'll eventually end up in prison.

Where does criminal behavior begin?

Criminal behavior usually begins at home and extends into the classroom, then finally toward society. These individuals usually begin acting up during their preteen years as they go in and out of juvenile centers. While in custody, if the juvenile offender is subjected to repetitive criticism by authority figures, his or her rebelliousness will continue to develop. In other words, repetitive criticisms fuel the Rebel Child into committing more crimes against society.

How did the offender's criminal behavior develop?

Chances are these individuals were exposed most of his or her life to caregivers who were both critical and rebellious themselves. In other words, individuals who are subjected to repetitive criticism, physical or emotional abuse will be at risk to have a dominant Critical Parent and Rebel Child to carry on the cycle of abuse to their off spring.

You mean I can't yell or criticize my kids when I'm a n g r y ?

If you choose to use your Critical Parent and Rebel Child on your children, you'll fuel his or her Critical Parent and Rebel Child against you. You'll get what you dish out. It's a vicious cycle. It's a no win situation. The bottom line is to avoid using the Critical Parent and the Rebel Child period when you are angry. Instead, focus on using your Adult to state you are angry. It's okay to be angry, but it's not okay to act out your anger on your children. Use your Nurturing Parent and your Adult to calm your Rebel Child down. Use positive self-talk to get in control of your emotions by saying, *I'm going to walk away and calm down. I can handle this problem in a calm and rational manner.*

What can I do to help individuals with a dominate Rebel Child develop into a responsible citizen?

Facilitate positive environments at home to shrink the Rebel Child and Critical Parent characters. Provide positive role models to help them develop their Nurturing Parent, Adult, and Responsible Child. It would be a matter of exposing theses individuals to nurturing role models, who would in turn teach them how to recognize, regulate, and replace their aggressive emotions for rational and logical thinking. If you can't be a Nurturing Parent, sign your children up for after school youth programs so they can get the exposure from another's Nurturing Parent and Adult. It doesn't matter who teaches your child how to control their behavior, or nurtures and loves them—the bottom line is they need exposure to positive role models to be successful in life.

If you are a parent of a child who needs help, you may not have the qualifications to help (meaning balance between characters). You too may need exactly what your child is missing out on—confidence and the ability to accept and show love. You may need to seek balance for your "self" in order to help your child seek balance in his or her life.

Does punishment rehabilitate criminals?

No, according to this methodology harsh punishment coming from a Critical Parent will not rehabilitate the offender. Punishment from the Critical Parent will only fuel the aggressive Rebel Child. The Rebel Child needs to be dealt with in an Adult manner, holding the individual responsible for his or her behavior. This individual must be taught problem solving skills, such as mediation, negotiation, and emotional regulation. The offenders need an infusion of respect and love, so they in turn learn to love and respect others.

"Tommy, I'm glad you came to me for help.
I'd be happy to work with you after school."

Are juveniles easier to rehabilitate?

There is hope for the juvenile offender because they are still in the process of character development and their exposure to institutional negativism has been less than the adult offender. The hope is that his or her caregivers take responsibility by seeking help for themselves. If caregivers begin taking an active role in their juvenile's character development – there is hope. These juveniles need the appreciation of nurturing and respectful individuals who can role model effective Adult responsibility.

What can we do personally to help our youth?

Be a positive role model. As a country, it's everyone's responsibility to embrace its youth. Don't assume you're not responsible because you aren't a parent. We are all role models.

SUMMARY

So, who's driving your bus? After reading this book, you ought to be able to answer this question. In addition to answering this question for yourself, you'll be able to help others understand who might be driving their bus. Now that you can recognize each of the five distinct characters, you can understand the meaning of internal conflict.

Accepting who you are this moment will help you assess what you need to do—to seek emotional balance. Emotional balance comes by knowing what particular character needs to develop more, and what character needs to take a vacation. It's in this achievement of balance between your five characters that you'll find peace and serenity.

Get in control of who's driving your bus… your life will be free of stress and internal conflict forever. — Cheryl

How can you get in touch with me?

I welcome your comments and questions on the content of this book. If you're over 18 years of age and would like to receive one-on-one, personal empowerment strategies in the areas of parenting, relationship building, individual or work related problems.

Please email me at cgallegos614@gmail.com.

Help A Friend . . .

Pass this book on with love & peace.

www.ingramcontent.com/pod-product-compliance
Lightning Source LLC
La Vergne TN
LVHW091154080426
835509LV00006B/680